The Atonement
A thought for each day of the year

Philip M. Hudson

Copyright 2020 by Philip M. Hudson.

Published 2020.

Printed in the United States of America.

All rights reserved.

No portion of this book may be reproduced, stored in a retrieval system, or transmitted in any form or by any means - electronic, mechanical, photocopy, recording, scanning, or other - except for brief quotations in critical reviews or articles, without the prior written permission of the author.

ISBN 978-1-950647-33-0

Illustrations - Google Images.

This book may be ordered from online bookstores.

Publishing Services by BookCrafters
Parker, Colorado.
www.bookcrafters.net

Table of Contents

Acknowledgements...i
Preface..v
Introduction..vii

A Thought For Each Day Of The Year...1
About The Author..367
By The Author..369
What More Can I Say?...373

Hell is really a heavenly reformatory that has been designed to improve the quality of our nature. It is a penitentiary where faith can still convict us of our sins. It was designed by God to help disobedient spirits recognize that Jesus Christ is the Mediator of the Covenant through His Atonement. In D&C 76, we learn that the Gospel was taught to the spirits kept in that prison. If, while there, they exercise their agency and accept not only Christ, but also the fullness of His Gospel, is it within the realm of possibility that they might also inherit celestial glory with the Saints. Surely, this is why we build temples and, without prejudice, perform vicarious work for all of our kindred dead.

Acknowledgements

In this volume, I have attributed quotations to original authors whenever possible, as well as when I have editorialized their ideas. In many cases, however, my language will naturally reflect the teachings of leaders and members of The Church of Jesus Christ of Latter-day Saints.

The list of those who have contributed to this book is endless. As I have organized my own thoughts, I have realized how heavily I have borrowed from the towering examples of those who, over the years, have been my mystical mentors, my sensible chaperones, my spiritual guides, my surrogate saviors, my compassionate critics, and everything in between.

They are my avatars, manifestations of deity in bodily forms, my na'vi, the visionaries, who communicate with God on a level to which I can only aspire, and my tsaddik, whom I esteem as intuitive interpreters of biblical law and scripture. They are my divine teachers incarnate. They have offered listening ears, extended open arms, lifted my spirits, shown me the way, stretched my mind, reinforced my faith, strengthened my testimony, helped me to discover my wings, given immaterial support, provided of their means, emboldened me with words of encouragement, cheered me on with wise counsel, taught me humility, been there to steady me, soothed my troubled soul, stepped in to nurture me, led me to fountains of living water, wet my parched lips with inspired counsel, and bound up my wounds.

When I think of the influence of a multitude of angels thinly disguised as my family, friends, and peers, I remember the words of Sir Isaac Newton, who, when pressed to reveal the great secret behind his accomplishments, simply replied: "I stood on the shoulders of giants." Of course, at the end of the day, I alone am responsible for the content of this volume. But I hope my interpretations of principles and doctrine will cultivate your interest to dig deeper into the themes woven into this tapestry, by turning to the scriptures and seeking inspiration from the Spirit. My only goal is to help you to expand your insights into the telestial mile markers, the terrestrial truths, and the celestial guidelines that accompany each of us during our quest for enlightenment as we embrace the Atonement.

God's children
who have grown to appreciate
His spiritual stature will use the
password of "Atonement" to get past
Security at the portal of heaven. As they
approach His throne, they will look back
to witness the transcendent beauty of the gate
through which they, as heirs of the kingdom, have
entered, which will be "like unto circling flames of
fire; Also the blazing throne of God, wherein" there
shall be "seated the Father and the Son." And the
"beautiful streets of that kingdom," shall have
"the appearance of being paved with gold."
(D&C 137:2-4). Thus, is described in
beautiful imagery, the promises of
our covenants, that are only
made possible through
the Atonement of
Christ.

Preface

I love to learn by reading the scriptures, and I often think of St. Hilary, who wrote in the third century: "Scripture consists not in what we read, but in what we understand." In each of the musings within this volume, I have consistently tried to find a scriptural foundation and a spiritual confirmation as I put my pen to paper.

I am continually reminded of Nephi's counsel to press forward with complete dedication and steadfastness, or confidence with a firm determination in Christ, having a perfect brightness of hope, or perfect faith, and charity, or a love of God and of all men. If we do this, feasting upon the word of Christ, or receiving strength and nourishment as we ponder the doctrines of the kingdom, and particularly the doctrine of Atonement, and as we then endure to the end in righteousness, we shall have eternal life, which is the greatest of God's gifts. (See 2 Nephi 31:20).

It is with love, then, that I extend to you the invitation to enjoy this omnibus of random thoughts. Embrace it at face value, and use its observations relating to baptism as a springboard to your own personal plateaus of discovery, as you are taught by the Spirit to move in the direction of your dreams.

The golden cobblestones of a stairway to the stars are illuminated by the principles of true conversion. These point us in the direction of the recognition of our iniquity, and then to a deep godly sorrow for our sins. Next comes inescapable suffering and torment that stimulates an appeal to the Savior, with an awakening understanding of the Atonement. After our baptism, comes the remission of our sins, spiritual enlightenment, and great joy. This motivates us to pursue a lifestyle of righteousness and service that is punctuated by our weekly observance of the Sacrament of the Lord's Supper. Each time this occurs, the endless loop cycles one more time, but it is calibrated to a higher plane of spiritual awareness.

Introduction

If they are fortunate, novice quilters quickly learn a bit of wisdom from the Amish, who make some of the finest quilts in the world. On purpose, the Amish build mistakes into their projects, because they believe that any attempt on their part to design and produce a flawless creation would be a mockery of God, Who alone is perfect. The humility of the Amish makes me think of my own weak attempts to put the thoughts expressed in this omnibus to paper. In His infinite wisdom, God knows very well that I do not need to consciously plan on lacing my efforts with errors. That will come quite naturally, without the need for me to intentionally contribute to my short-comings.

Perhaps this serendipitous collection of musings will do little more than help to define quirks in my personality. Each of us is different, and many things, including our family and friends, the circumstances in which we find ourselves, the quality of our education, and our own personalities, inspire and mold our oral and written expressions. I would like to think that, in this text, all of these influences have been encouraging, affirmative, and constructive.

The reflections within this tome leave the door ajar for the reader, to allow shafts of the light of understanding to creep in. If, as I have expressed my thoughts, I mis-stated myself a few times, or flat-out got it wrong, I ask the patient indulgence and gentle correction of the reader.

Too often, I realize that my communications can be "carefully disguised with hypocrisy and glittering words," as Einstein put it. Although I do fancy myself a wordsmith, I have tried to avoid pedestrian expressions, idle language, and lazy scholarship. I do not pretend to be an authority on the doctrine of the Atonement, inasmuch as I believe that we are all works in progress, but if you find the factual tone of a particular musing disengaging, the truth is that I typically experienced a deep personal involvement in my interpretation of the principles that illuminated its meaning.

In any event, when you open this volume, I hope you ponder these minute musings with as much enjoyment as I have experienced while creating them.

We are baptized
that those who have
died without having had
the opportunity to hear about
The Plan of Salvation might also
partake of eternal life. The Atonement
is the gold standard not only for those who
are the living, but also of vicarious work for
the dead. In our day, the Savior has given the
members of His Church the commission to follow
His example, and to act in behalf of the dead; of
those who are unable to perform saving ordinances
for themselves, since they have passed beyond the
veil and are living, without tangible bodies,
in the Spirit World, while they await their
own spiritual renewal, redemption
and resurrection.

All of us are repeatedly faced with occasions when withdrawals must be made from our spiritual bank accounts. When we respond to the Spirit, Who drives us to our knees to help us to recognize the awesome power of the Atonement, we put the principle of repentance to its ultimate test. But we do not write checks that can't be cashed. We realize that only after regular deposits have been made over a period of time, can we rely upon the cornucopia of comfort created by the cushion of confidence that is a currency flowing from conduct that is consistent with the core curriculum of contrition.

Maybe
The Plan
will leave God's
disobedient children
in the Spirit Prison of The
Unjust only long enough for
them to recognize the error of
their ways, and to motivate them
to make behavioral changes that are
balanced with the teachings, ordinances,
and covenants of the Gospel. Recognizing
their transgressions, such individuals might
be required to pay directly for the sins they
had committed in mortality that had fallen
outside the merciful sphere of influence of
the Atonement. Such punishment would be
eternally and endlessly in harmony with
the Law of Mercy, and it would seem to
also satisfy the demands of Justice,
allowing God' perfect Plan to
move forward in harmony
with His bold mission
statement.

If we delay our quest to rely upon the power of the Atonement until we have become spiritually blinded to the Holy Ghost, we will become subject to the spirit of the devil. If he captures our hearts, they will become mutated, and be stony and cold, and we will lose the capacity to distinguish good from evil, virtue from vice, and light from darkness. If we become so audacious that we switch the sunshine that has been generated by the foundation of faith for the wintry weather of worldliness, the Spirit of the Lord will withdraw, to visit warmer climes. Then, we will see how Satan's icy breath can be sucked into the vortex we have created for him.

A number of
the chapters in the
story of our lives have
already been set to type,
and we don't know how many
remain to be written. But this we
know: The fairytale was created by
Heavenly Father, and we must honor
its premise that we are His sons and
daughters. We cannot start over and
make a new beginning, but we can
begin now, and with the help of a
talented and gifted Ghostwriter,
Whose nom du plume is the Holy
Ghost, write new endings to
chapters entitled "Faith,"
and "The Atonement
of Christ."

Those
who question
the Atonement
should know that
we, and not the Lord,
are already on trial. He
will be present at the Bar of
Justice, to weigh the evidence
that is for us and against us. Our
previous acceptance or rejection of
the doctrine of the kingdom of God,
and how we embraced it, will determine
our reward or punishment. A court date
for the upcoming proceedings has already
been docketed. It will follow shortly on
the heels of our mortal experience, and
will be handled with neither prejudice
nor preference. We should begin the
preparation of our legal brief now,
that the motion we submit for
mercy might be summarily
granted by a Judge Who,
at the end of the day,
is kindhearted.

Those who
turn their backs to
the Atonement of Jesus
Christ are left to grope about
in the dark and gasp for a breath
of celestial air. The faithful keep their
faces oriented toward the light of Christ
so they will always feel the gentle breeze
of heaven on their cheeks. At the same
time, because the shadows are always
behind them, they might not even be
aware of the encroaching gloom.
At the very least, they will no
longer be afraid of
the dark.

The Gospel
of Jesus Christ
shepherds us through
the growing pains and the
mental, emotional, physical,
and spiritual unsteadiness that
are related to early childhood
development. However, until our
behavior matures so that it is in
harmony with the Atonement, the
freedom that exists outside the
sphere of the moral element of
responsibility that is faith must
inevitably forge our fetters
and lead us into bondage.
The blueprint that is the
Gospel is, on the other
hand, the perfect Law
of liberty.

The demands that
are placed on us by the
Atonement have the capacity
to generate relationship capital,
when we feel ourselves being carried
to heaven's gate, as upon the wings of
eagles. At the same time, we understand
that the insolvency of Satan's seduction
cannot be mitigated by a third-party
bailout. The only financially sound
solution to his nepotism is to use
the priceless bargaining chips
of the Atonement of
Jesus Christ.

Our failure to repent is yet
another example of rebellion against
the Atonement of Jesus Christ. We must
recall that in the wake of the insurgency
by Lucifer that resulted in war in heaven,
there were grave consequences for the losers
that were both painful and eternally damaging
in their scope. For those of us who prevailed at
the conclusion of that conflict, we were able
to continue to grow in grace, that we might
progress in stature in our second estate,
until, through the Atonement of Christ,
we could move on to our third estate
where we would reach the pinnacle
of achievement, wherein The Plan
would have nurtured within us
both the image and the
likeness of our
Father.

Without
faith in God,
some see things as they
are, and ask: "Why?" But the
focused faithful dream things that
never were, and thru the power of the
Atonement of Christ, ask: "Why not?" They
work thru their problems, instead of skirting
around them. Our reliance upon the Atonement
of Jesus Christ compels us to be disciplined in
our commitment, with sustained effort and an
ongoing responsibility with accountability. The
Lord has given us two ends: One to think
with and the other to sit on. Which one
we use will determine how well we
do in life. In other words:
Heads we win, and tails
we lose.

Those who, thru no fault of their own, have been denied the chance in this life to embrace the Gospel, will be judged according to their more limited understanding of the doctrines and principles that are related to deliverance. Therefore, when they stand before the Judgment Bar, they will vary in their accountability to law. The reach of the Atonement lies in its ability to bless our lives, without regard to individual circumstances. It is both infinite and eternal in its scope, because each of us must play the hand we have been dealt. The Lord, however, has resources that are sufficient to cover all of our bets.

Paul knew what it meant for the Lord to ask us to go the second mile. He labored among the Corinthian Saints, whom he was pleased to discover had a working relationship with the laws and the ordinances of the Gospel. He characterized their previous expressions of faith as having been written upon "tables of stone." That is all well and good, but he hinted that there exists another order of mind, a connection that can be ours if we will embrace the Atonement of Jesus Christ: "Ye are manifestly declared to be the epistle of Christ ministered by us, written not with ink, but with the Spirit of the living God; not in tables of stone, but in fleshy tables of the heart." (2 Corinthians 3:3).

The Devil,
who has always been
a consummate con man,
a master deceiver, and was
a liar from the beginning, even
now continues his efforts to foil the
execution of The Plan of Salvation and
the education of all of God's children, by
the substitution of his counterfeit proposal.
That desperate and unworkable alternative
would have required neither repentance nor
an Atonement by a Savior. Fortunately, at
the Council in Heaven, when both plans
were discussed, we were able to see
through his deception. Today, we
retain our eternal perspective
and our actions reflect our
continuing determination
to be disciples of
Christ.

Those who are not
currently worthy to enter
the House of the Lord cannot
come where Christ is. But, if they
are able to make behavioral changes,
and if they can modify their nature so
that as they mature their character more
fully reflects that of their Father, perhaps
then they will be invited to enjoy His hearth
and home, on earth and in heaven. Surely,
the story of the Prodigal Son, set against
the backdrop of the infinite and eternal
Atonement of Jesus Christ, lends its
support to the thesis that there are
seeds of greatness that can be
found within each of us, no
matter how broken we
may appear to be.

At first, it may
be the easier wrong
that appears to be more
convenient, but that is only
because it harmonizes with the
values of Babylon. Worldliness is
all around us. If we cannot find the
stabilizing influence that is provided by
faith in the Atonement of Jesus Christ, our
moral equivocation can quickly turn into the
path of least resistance, until it become the
pattern of our conduct. Faith invites us to
trust in the divine design of our Father
in Heaven that is grounded upon the
Atonement of His Son. It nurtures
our belief that it is only in Him
that our lives can become
'fairy tales waiting to be
written by the hand
of God.'

One among many of the significant functions of the Holy Spirit is to bear a sacred witness of our honesty with God, as we repent with broken hearts. His unimpeachable witness is as a baptism of fire that puts the finishing touches on the Atonement of Jesus Christ. When Mercy intervenes to satisfy the demands of Justice and cancels the penalties that are associated with our sins, we are blessed to become holy and without spot, in a rite of purification. Though our "sins be as scarlet, they shall be as white as snow. Though they be red like crimson, they shall be as wool." (Isaiah 1:18).

The
Atonement
gives each of us
the opportunity to be
repetitively re-vitalized, as
we are re-introduced to that
magical kingdom where our hopes
and our dreams really do come true,
and we all live happily ever after. When
we wish upon the star of Jesus Christ, it
will make no difference who we are.
Anything that our hearts desire will
come to us. If we put the energy
of our souls into our dreams,
no request we have will
seem too extreme.

The Merciful Plan
of our Father requires that
we give up only our sins to merit
salvation through His boundless grace.
It is axiomatic that our exercise of free
will must be carried out in an atmosphere
that is fraught with danger. Unfortunately,
undesirable consequences will inevitably
follow with frustrating frequency. When
this occurs, it was ordained in heaven
before the creation of the world,
that their effects be mitigated
by the Atonement of
Jesus Christ.

Those
of weak will, who
are swift in running to
mischief, forfeit their desire to
repent, although they may not even
be consciously aware of it. They lose
their focus, just as eyesight may be lost
over time. First they will squint, and then
they might hold the page a bit closer or a
little further away, compensating for their
inability to see clearly. It could be either
the printed page or their integrity that
they cannot read. But in the latter
case, without the clarity that is
provided by the Atonement,
there is a compromise of
character crippling
proportion.

If we
postpone our
pursuit of the holy
grail of the Atonement
until our vision fades and
we have become blinded to the
Light of Christ, we will surrender
ourselves to the spirit of the devil.
When he captures our hearts, he will
mutate them to become stony and
cold; we will lose the capacity to
distinguish good from evil and
light from darkness. When we
exchange the sunshine that is
generated by the foundation
of faith for wintry weather
and worldliness, the Spirit
of the Lord will withdraw
to visit warmer climes.
Then, the icy breath of
Satan will be sucked
into the vortex we
have created
for him.

After the Fall, the
portal to Eden may have swung
shut, but as it did so, another door
opened that introduced Adam and Eve
to a secret garden accessible only to those
who would utilize the key of the Atonement
thru baptism by immersion for the remission
of their sins. They would have experience
with good as well as with evil, with light
as well as with darkness, with virtue as
as well as with vice, with health as
well as with sickness, and with
pleasure as well as with
pain, all in the white
hot crucible of
experience.

Our godly walk (see D&C 20:69) is only made possible because of the Atonement, which can save us from our natural state of carnality, sensuality, and devilish inclinations. It activates the Law of Mercy, which mitigates for those who conform to its requirements the effects of the first Law, that demands Justice. It lifts us to a state of holiness, spirituality, angelic innocence, and happiness. It prepares us to feel comfortable in our heavenly home, where we will find that we are in the pleasant company of legions of angels who will serenade us with lullabies that expresses love for us in the rapturous language of the Celestial Kingdom.

Sometimes all too quickly, and at other times agonizingly slowly, those who have sold their souls to the Devil for a mess of pottage are dragged down to a hell on earth that is of their own construction. Their bad habits are the result of repetitively impulsive behaviors that, in a rising tide of wickedness, continually erode away at the foundations of agency. They are fettered by the chains of compulsions. They realize too late that unlimited freedom leads to tyranny. The Holy Ghost, however, has the power to lead them to the Atonement's path of safety, and to the Savior's perfect law of liberty.

The Atonement of Jesus Christ can assure us that we will be resurrected and will live forever. But it asks us to do a bit more. We must organize ourselves, and "prepare every needful thing; and establish a house, even a house of prayer, a house of fasting, a house of faith a house of learning, a house of glory, (and) a house of order." (D&C 88:119). In effect, we must create and maintain a house that has been dedicated to God, that we might inherit not only immortality, which is freely given to all, but also the greater gift of eternal life, which is reserved for the obediently faithful.

It is only the Atonement of our Savior Jesus Christ that can unshackle us from the disagreeable demands that, in the absence of Mercy, would have otherwise been imposed upon all of us by Justice. While darkness is the conjoined twin of misery, the obedience of faith frees us to embrace the truth, to make intelligent choices, to perform purposefully, to carry on convincingly, and to progress persistently. In short, we may rise above all of the cares of the world through His sacrifice for our sins of omission and commission, and all of our other shortcomings that lie somewhere in between.

How many times
have we read about,
or even witnessed, cultural
collapse because a faithless society
has decayed from within? In every case,
iniquity follows those who yield themselves
"unto the power of Satan." (3 Nephi 7:5). The
world does not seem to be able to understand
that Lucifer was a first-grade dropout whose
influence was the companion of anarchy. As
his disciples do today, he denied the power
of the Atonement and he demeaned the
idea that the intelligent application of
knowledge could help us to work
out our salvation before God,
angels, and witnesses.

In an arduous
repentance process,
we find the strength we
need thru the infinite power
of the Atonement of Jesus Christ.
As we continue to seek the Lord while
He may be found, a constant companion
will instruct us how we may become better
engaged in fashioning defensive weapons
in our armory of thought. It is with these
tools that the Spirit will guide us and
direct us. He will show us just what
we need to do in order to build
our heavenly fortifications of
love, joy, strength, service,
compassion, testimony,
conversion, and
peace.

Those who
embrace the Atonement
of Jesus Christ embark upon
a journey that is as old as time.
Their faith will introduce them to a
procedure with which they may not be
familiar, even that of a spiritual heart
transplant. As they face a bright future
after they have been born again in a
newness of life, carefully prescribed
anti-rejection protocols need to be
followed, in order to protect and
preserve the new organs that
are steadily beating in
their chests.

Sometimes all too quickly, and at other times agonizingly slowly, those who have sold their souls to the Devil for a mess of pottage are dragged down to a hell on earth that is of their own construction. Their bad habits are the result of repetitively impulsive behaviors that, in a rising tide of wickedness, continually erode away at the foundations of their agency. They are restrained by the heavy chains of their compulsions. Only when it is too late do they realize that, without the safety net of the Atonement of Jesus Christ, the freedom, or more accurately, the license that they had so rashly pursued must inevitably lead to tyranny.

If we do
not forgive others
their trespasses against us,
we will find that the influence
of the Spirit, that would normally
burn as a fire within our hearts, has
been quenched. The Atonement itself
will have lost its capability to purge
sin from our own troubled souls. If
we persist in slinging dirt, we will
inevitably lose ground. We must
change our nature to become
new creatures in Christ, and
we must be light upon our
feet, to quickly follow
His supernal example
of forgiveness.

We press on
in faith, in the
light of the Spirit,
and are rewarded by
the Atonement with an
illumination of Gospel
principles that will bathe
our minds in a cascade of
the celestial diamond dust
of inspiration and revelation.
We are resolute in our resolve
to repent, and we renounce our
iniquity, for the Spirit reminds
us that it is nothing less than
a frightening after-image of
the rebellion of Lucifer
when he stood before
the Council in
heaven.

It we look at the
pillars of creation in the
context of the Atonement, our
feeble efforts to comprehend the
universe in which we live may help
us to understand ourselves. If we ask,
what is its origin, or what is its ultimate
destiny, we are really asking where did
we come from, and where are we going.
When we discover the answers to these
questions, we will better understand
why we are here. This will prepare
us to embrace the expansive scope
of The Plan of Salvation and the
sacrifice of the Savior. This
catalyzing knowledge will
propel us on a journey
of faith into the
cosmos.

The reach of the Atonement of Christ extends so far that it has power to neutralize the sins of the best of us and the worst of us; both the living and the dead. There are no limits to its temporal and eternal influence. It simply waits upon our initiative to manifest its energy through the vicarious work of the Atonement, and through our vicarious work performed in the temple, to transport us, together with our kindred dead, into a harmony with the heavens and the presence of God.

As we
learn to rely on
the Atonement, the
righteousness of our
efforts will be revealed
in spectacular simplicity
and plainness. The walls of
opposition to our purposeful
repentance will crumble and
fall away. In our efforts, the
Lord will comfort and succor
us with the Bread of Life. As we
journey through the harsh and
unforgiving environment of
Babylon, seeking the Lord
while He may be found,
oases will spring up
in the desert and
living water will
slake our
thirst.

It is only
our profound obedience
and recurring repentance that
release us from the bondage of
sin and qualify us by worthiness to
enjoy the blessings of the temple. The
Atonement of Jesus Christ, which is the
centerpiece of the instruction that we
receive in the endowment, allows us
to overcome our limitations while
unleashing the powers of heaven.
It shatters the glass ceiling of
death by breaking its bands,
for all who have ever
lived on the earth,
and for all who
ever will.

When the
Spirit nurtures
the focus of our
undivided attention
on The Plan of Salvation,
we will have discovered the
unlimited energy source of the
cosmos. We will "discard the poor
lenses of our bodies, and peer thru
the telescope of truth into the infinite
reaches of immortality." (Helen Keller).
On the other hand, if we fail to nurture
our faith in the Great and Eternal Plan
of Redemption, if our engines stall for
lack of power, we may find ourselves
caught up in a flat spin from which
there may be no recovery.

If we dare to make
the choice to remain in a
state of rebellion against the
power of the Atonement to save
us from our sins, the fruit of the
Tree of Life will remain just beyond
our reach, even tho, out of curiosity,
we now and then will try to take a
bite. If we never raise our eyes to
search eternal horizons, the world
before us will appear as nothing
more than a barren desert that
is devoid of refreshing oases,
the welcome shade of trees,
and an abundance of well
watered gardens. If we
cannot muster faith to
nourish the word of
God, it will not
be able to
sustain
us.

Standing in
opposition to the
light of the Spirit is
a darkness that has the
potential to cover the earth,
and gross darkness the people.
Without the influence of the Holy
Ghost to intervene in our behalf by
introducing us to the Atonement, we
would be held captive by the source of
that gloom, to rise no more. The Devil,
who was a liar from the beginning, even
now continues his efforts to foil The Plan
by the substitution of his own counterfeit,
unworkable alternative that would not
require repentance or the Atonement.
Fortunately, in the setting of the
Council in Heaven, we could see
through his deception. Because
of the guidance of the Spirit,
sent by our Heavenly Father
to accompany us on our
journey thru mortality,
we still do today.

It is
instructive to
think of Joseph's
coat of many colors
as a metaphor for the
fabric of our faith, sewn
by our Heavenly Father. We
can visualize how each thread
has been individually tailored to
suit our circumstances; to represent,
not the drab monotone of the world,
but a true Technicolor DreamCoat that
signifies the glories and the riches of
dazzling eternal worlds. These fall
within our reach only because the
Atonement stretches our bolts
of cloth far beyond their
normal dimensions.

The
Atonement
of Jesus Christ
binds us to heaven by
creating a pulsing stream
of inspiration whose flow has
has no temporal boundary and
no spatial limitation. Thru His
sacrifice, we are at one with
the mind and the will of
our Heavenly Father.

When our hearts
are hardened against
the invitation that has been
extended by the Lord to repent,
it is as though our portion has been
diminished further and further, until
our defenses against the aggressive
tactics of the Devil crumble, and
we are left to fight our battles
alone, without the protection
that could have been ours
thru the Atonement
of Jesus Christ.

No matter
that we may, for
all intents and purposes,
be dead weight. It is in the
sacrifice of the Savior that He
exhibits the strength to carry us
until we have been revitalized to
walk without becoming weary, and
run without fainting. We need the
the light from the Atonement
to disperse the darkness
that encroaches upon
our world.

Those who
settle for the moral
mediocrity of character
crippling personality flaws
can never get enough of what
they don't need, because what
they don't need will never
satisfy them. Whether we
know it or not, what
we all need is the
Atonement in
our lives.

When
we are born
again thru the
Atonement, our
orientation is more
toward the expansive
laws of the hidden world
than it is to the restrictive
boundaries of our physical
surroundings. Thereby, we
find that our spirits can
be exercised as they
are nurtured by
repentance.

Repentance is
just the prescription
the Doctor ordered to
treat the religious fever
that elevates our testimony
temperature enough to get
our juices flowing with a
visceral appreciation of
the sacrifice of the
Savior thru His
Atonement.

It
is our
faith in the
Atonement that
helps us to redefine
and redesign what had
heretofore been stumbling
blocks. They are repurposed
into the very stepping stones
that are needed to conquer
our doubts, strengthen our
confidence, and conquer
the obstacles we will all
encounter along the
pathways of our
progression.

We recognize that
the Atonement of Jesus
Christ has worked its magic,
when the Spirit of the Lord
falls upon us, and we are
filled with joy. When we
are clean, we enjoy a
peace of conscience
that will defy any
explanation.

There will
always exist among us
those stubborn souls who
doggedly refuse to repent by
confessing their sins to Deity.
They persistent in looking to
gods of wood and stone that
may only temporarily soothe
their temporal and spiritual
trauma. But, ultimately, it
is only the Atonement of
Christ that will redeem
them from their self
induced misery.

The
influence
of the Light of
Christ encourages
us to set our sights
upon the pole-star of
the Atonement, that was
designed by God to point
us to a higher plateau of
progress. We must work,
but our lunch is free.
It has been provided
by the Savior of
the world.

The Atonement teaches us to be patient, even in the face of challenges when our portion seems unfair, when our difficulties seem unreasonable, and when the proportions of the problems looming before us seem daunting.

If we examine it closely, woven within the fabric of the material that makes up the tapestry of Atonement, there are sometimes "dark threads that are as needful in the Weaver's skillful hand as the threads of gold and silver, in the pattern He has planned."
(B. Franklin).

In our stressful and complex world, we often see through a glass darkly, making it very difficult for us to know how to harness the energy of the elusive equations found within the powerful doctrine of the Atonement of Jesus Christ.

The brilliantly crafted doctrine of Atonement has been designed as a celestial thermostat that easily mitigates the volatility of the telestial tempests that regularly sweep across our lives.

We may be very surprised to find that our enduring to the end simply involves mastery of two principles that are tied to the Savior's Atonement: Repentance for our own sins, and our own forgiveness of the trespasses by others.

The HazMat
Protocol of the
Atonement has been
written into The Plan to
detoxify us from the cares
and conditioning influences
of the world, and from the
homogenization process
that occurs as we are
worn down by the
vicissitudes
of life.

It is Christ's Atonement that generates repetitive opportunities to smell the delicious aroma of the bread of life that has been baking in a celestial oven. In anticipation of a buttered slice, we steadily move along on the path that carries us closer to the threshold of our heavenly home.

The Atonement of Jesus Christ is like a stethoscope that has the ability to detect our cardiac vital capacity. When our hearts have broken in contrition, we are able to identify the steady sinus rhythm that is our substantiation of the congruence that exists between repentance, forgiveness, and the greater light of God.

The Atonement
has the potential to order
our chaotic world, to bless us
with clarity rather than confusion,
to teach us how to achieve fluency in
the language of the Spirit, and to educate
those who are functionally illiterate in
terms of Gospel scholarship, so that
all might be equally mesmerized
by the redemptive power
of Jesus Christ.

The great Plan that
was created by our Father
in Heaven envisions a utopian
society, but it is also pragmatic.
It anticipated our weaknesses and
provided us with the Atonement as
a practical solution for those of
us (meaning all of us) whose
agency would lead them
away from the Rod
of Iron.

I will go before your face," the Lord has promised. "I will be on your right hand, and on your left, and my Spirit shall be in your hearts, and mine angels round about you, to bear you up." (D&C 84:88). With such assurance, how could we think to turn away from the Atonement of Christ by persisting in our wicked ways, and by flying solo, without a parachute?

The Atonement of Jesus Christ blesses us to employ intrinsic countermeasures to wicked imaginations. Our behavior is driven by altruism, self-denial, self-discipline, self-restraint, and self-sacrifice. These all come as we listen with our hearts to the promptings of the Spirit that are as the quiet whisper of a gentle breeze that caresses our cheeks.

We
are slow to
mischief each time
we exercise our ability
to look beyond telestial
temptations and temporal
trivia; when we possess the
will to adjust our perspective
so that the Atonement becomes
a powerful motivator for good
as it removes the stain of sin
from the tapestry that is the
tableau of our lives in the
telestial winter of the
lone and dreary
world.

It is in
the Atonement
of Jesus Christ that
our innate longing to be
clean finds expression in the
celestial sparks that are struck
off the divine anvil of God, that
ignite our desire to repent and to be
baptized. The Atonement fashions, not
only immortal love, but also eternal
life. The eventual death of the body
is a horizon that is nothing, save
the limit of our sight, and we
perish only when we have
lost the vision of our
heavenly home.

Those who
decline the offer of
the riches of eternity that
might have been unfolded to
their view through the power of
the Atonement are doomed to
live their lives in scarcity of
their basic spiritual needs.
They live beneath the
poverty level, but
may not even
be aware
of it.

Those who can
really appreciate the power
of the ordinance of baptism are
able to visualize the Celestial Kingdom.
They use the Atonement of Christ to move
in its direction. They follow the admonition
of the Savior: "Seek ye first the kingdom
of God, and his righteousness; and all
these things shall be added unto
you." (Matthew 6:33).

In our day, we are witnessing how electronic media can interfere with our relationship with the Holy Ghost, Whose influence is vital to the execution of the celestial doctrine of the Atonement.

The endowment
soften our telestial
tendencies and creates
an impenetrable shield of
faith. The Plan of Salvation,
of which it testifies, provides a
sounding board against which we
may discern between the polarized
opposites that seek our attention.
The Atonement, which lies at its
center, describes the difference
between joy and its worldly
counterfeits, and strikes
familiar chords within
our heartstrings.

Our
abiding faith
in the divine Plan
of our Father in Heaven
is confirmed in the temple,
where we learn that it has been
designed to bring us back into His
kingdom after we have grown up unto
the Lord, have spiritually matured,
and have demonstrated that the
basis of our hope of salvation
is in His Atonement, and
that alone.

The power
of Jesus Christ
is manifest in our
temple covenants, and
our solemn oaths trigger
a cleansing. The process of
our sanctification through the
Atonement allows us to draw near
to God's throne in heaven, realizing
that He will bestow upon our heads
the blessings we need, instead
of those that we thought
we had wanted.

Our understanding
of the pre-mortal existence,
as it unfolds in the endowment,
sanctifies life, dignifies individual
effort, and rewards achievement.
Most importantly, it recognizes the
Atonement as the pivotal center
of the perfect Plan of
Salvation.

Our finest hour are when unexpected challenges are met with extraordinary effort. Just like the Seven Dwarfs, when we embrace the tenets of the temple, we whistle while we work out our salvation, because of the miracle of the Atonement. We learn how our Heavenly Father has linked our own efforts to those of His Son. Happiness, as it turns out, is the object and design of our existence, and it will be the end thereof, if we follow the path of repentance that leads to it.

All of
us will be
tested by trials
and temptations,
and we will make
mistakes. But we will
rise above our failures
because of our love of the
Savior, and His Atonement. It
is in the next act that all the
mysteries will be solved, all the
pieces of the puzzle will be put in
their proper place, all the confusion
that had aforetime tormented us will
be put to rest, and everything will be
made right. For that to occur, we
need to be up and about, starting
right now, by making our way
past every obstacle on the
path that leads to the
feet of the Savior.

God's Plan was designed as a locomotive to help us to enjoy our ride thru life. We board that train that is bound for glory. We have a first-class ticket, so that the dust, delays, sidetracks, smoke, cinders, and jolts will be a lot more comfortable. The conductor of that train is Jesus Christ, Who provides significant relief from the pressures of the journey, by punching our tickets with His Atonement.

We
cannot expect
to comprehend the
language of the Spirit
until we have paid the price.
We may dismiss its whisperings
as nothing more than a breeze that
causes a gentle rustle of the leaves
in the forest that is our conscience.
It may sound pleasant to our ears,
but its quiet counsel will remain
maddeningly elusive until we
have done all that we can to
merit the companionship of
this gift that we receive
thru the Atonement
of Christ.

Since there
is opposition in
all things, even as there
is faith, so must there also
be its worldly counterpart. In
our day, the grip of fear paralyzes
many of God's children. Today, more
than ever, we need the Holy Ghost. We
need the assurance of peace, that our
lives are moving in the direction of
our dreams, and that it is thru the
Atonement that we are given the
tools we all need to hitch our
wagons to the stars that have
been created by God to
define the pathway to
the heavens.

Telestial
E.M.T.s are at a
total loss for diagnosis,
while the supernal gift of the
Atonement provides a virtual war
chest of therapies for cold, stony,
and hard hearts. Our faith in the
merits of Jesus Christ is the
remedy of choice for
reconciliation.

It makes very little difference to our Father whether we are combating the influence of the Seven Deadly Sins, or the garden-variety of transgressions that we commit each day. The doctrine of the Atonement stipulates that we must go through a process of repentance before we are admitted into the Church thru baptism, and receive the Spirit.

We are baptized
because of our testimony
that the principles governing
the Fall of Adam, as well as the
Savior's Atonement, were "great and
eternal purposes (that) were prepared
from the foundation of the world."
(Alma 42:26). Our baptism itself
testifies that we understand
the significance of the
sacrifice of our
Redeemer.

It is in
this life that we
must prepare for our
reunion with our Father in
Heaven, by striving to become
pure and holy. Our participation in
the Sacrament as we seek the Spirit is
the tangible expression of our appeal
to the Savior to come to our rescue,
and in particular of our desire to
rely upon His Atonement, to heal
the self-inflicted damage that
has been caused by sin and
that is the consequence
of the weaknesses in
the armor of our
shields of
faith.

To
the great
relief of grieving
parents, the Atonement
affirms the innocence of
children. It was an integral
element of The Plan that was
ordained in the Council in Heaven
before the creation, that little ones
who would pass away before they had
reached the age of accountability would
be saved in eternal glory by the power
of our Savior and our Redeemer. His
influence extends to every corner
of the earth, from the beginning
of the world to the very end
of time. Truly, did He say:
"Suffer the little children
to come unto me."
(Mark 10:4).

It is to our
great advantage that
we become acquainted with
evil as well as with good, with
pain as well as with pleasure, and
with darkness as well as with light;
with error as well as with truth, and
with punishment for the infraction of
God's eternal laws, as well as with the
blessings that follow our obedience.
The Atonement of Jesus Christ gives
us the opportunity to profit from
all of these character-building
life experiences.

The fulcrum of our faith lies astride the doctrine of the Atonement, and on the principles of repentance and forgiveness, as well as on the ordinance of baptism. This trifecta just happen to be the polar opposite of life without light.

From the
liberating and
refreshing perspective
of Mercy, the Savior of the
world has negotiated with Justice
to purchase our sins with the legally
recognized currency of the Atonement.
His voluntary act of sacrifice is perfectly
balanced and attuned to accomplish the
task at hand, but it is augmented by
faith, repentance, baptism, the Gift
of the Holy Ghost, and finally, by
the Sacrament, which addresses
the renewal of the baptismal
covenant we have made
with our Heavenly
Father.

Our faith may as well be dead, without the accompanying work of repentance that is made possible by the Atonement, and continually fortified as we partake of the Sacrament. Our faith notwithstanding, we do not have the power to save ourselves from the unalterable demands of Justice. So Mercy might abound, our Heavenly Father created covenants that are linked to the ordinances of the Gospel.

The infinite
and eternal Atonement
of our Savior Jesus Christ
is the codicil to the best fire
insurance policy that could ever
have been written, indemnifying us
against the possibility of being burned
as stubble at the last day. As long as
we pay our premiums, we will receive
our immortal bodies as benefits of
the resurrection, so that we might
dwell in celestial burnings and
avoid being consumed. Such
is the power of The Plan
of our God.

When we
are dealing
with weaknesses
in our contractions
that push forward the
Lord's agenda, relying on
the power of the Atonement
and upon the Holy Ghost to be
our labor coach quickens us to
deliver our witness without the
danger of being overzealously
overbearing. It's just that we
may need a minimal dose
of spiritual pitosin to
jump start the
process.

While
repentance is
a fuel that fires
our determination
to follow the Savior,
His Atonement charges
our spiritual batteries by
energizing our vision with
an infinite perspective. With
an electrifying awareness, we
realize we can become holy
and without spot because
of our Lord's sacrifice
in our behalf.

Standing in
inarticulate opposition to the
grace of God is a darkness that is
so pervasive that it has the potential
to cover the earth, and gross darkness
the people. Without repentance, baptism,
and the Atonement of Christ, we would
be blinded by the evil source of that
melancholy and left destitute; to
hesitantly tap our way through
life, bereft of the power to
triumphantly rise in the
resurrection of the
just with the
Saints of
God.

With the
Atonement of Christ,
the arguably evil elements
of a Plan that, at first blush,
seemed to stand in opposition
to life have become the pathway
and portal to a joyful reunion
in the eternities, where we will
meet our families before the
pleasing bar of God at a
missionary reunion that
is unimaginable, at
least for now.

The Devil completely misread the situation that surrounded the Fall of Adam, and he misjudged the ability of the Redeemer of the world to save all of mankind thru the Atonement. All that has been necessary to restore purity to the sons and the daughters of Adam and Eve is the further light and knowledge that God promised to give us. The adversary never saw that one coming, but it is safe to say that it has made all the difference in the world. As Parley P. Pratt said: "I have received the holy anointing. I can never rest until the last enemy has been conquered, death is destroyed, and the truth reigns triumphant."

If we allow
ourselves to sink
into the quicksand of
carnality, and we lose the
wide-eyed innocence of youth,
our purity, and our holiness, we
will forfeit the happiness that can
only accompany untroubled souls,
thru the miracle of the Atonement
of the Redeemer of all mankind.
The peace of which He speaks is
not as the world gives, for it
is that of an unafraid heart
through the spirit of
reconciliation.

It was an integral
element of The Plan of Salvation,
ordained in the grand Council in Heaven
before the world was, that little children who
died before the age of accountability would be
saved in the Celestial Kingdom by the power of
the Atonement. "If not so, God is a partial
God, and also a changeable God, and
a respecter of persons; for how
many little children have
died without baptism!"
(Moroni 8:12).

When we have been
quickened by the Spirit,
we identify the source of
the life-giving water that is
offered, and we accept in our
hearts the sacrifice of the Savior,
manifest in His Atonement. When we
transgress, we speedily repent and
return unto God, to find favor in
His sight; to have our blessings,
that He is anxious to restore,
poured out once again
upon our heads.

It is nothing less than the unblemished innocence, simplicity, transparency, purity, and virtue of little children who are about to be baptized that blesses us with the optimism that the peace of God is within our reach. When we change our nature to be as they are, "submissive, meek, humble, patient, (and) full of love," the enticings of the Holy Spirit help us to put off the natural man and to become Saints through the Atonement of Christ.
(Mosiah 3:19).

The object and and design of our existence is that we might find happiness, peace, and rest; that we might obtain the blessings of the fathers, including the fruits of faith, which is baptism by immersion for the remission of our sins, through the Atonement of Christ. (See Moroni 8:11).

Our
engagement
with life in a forum
of free will propels us
onward toward immortality
and eternity, as long as we are
obedient to ordinances, covenants,
and the Atonement of Christ. These
are the devices that will keep the
sand of sin out of the gears
of the machine that was
created in heaven for
the making of
Gods.

Grace has the power to raise us up from physical death by the resurrection, and from spiritual death thru the Atonement of Christ. We receive the grace of God proportionately as we conform to His standard of personal righteousness that can only be found in the teachings of the Gospel of Jesus Christ.

We are accountable to God for our own actions, which will either destroy us or, thru faith in the Atonement, lift us into the embrace of angels to deify us, in strict accord with the doctrine of eternal progression. We cannot have it both ways, however. If we sow sparingly, we shall reap accordingly. On the other hand, if we sow bountifully, we shall also reap bountifully. (See 2 Corinthians 9:6).

The Atonement anticipated the shortcomings, the sins of omission, and the sins of commission that, from the beginning to the end of time, would be exasperatingly committed by men and women, and boys and girls. For, "as it is written, there is none righteous, no, not one." (Romans 3:10).

People think
that they can be
happy if they wander
and play, forgetting that
a key feature of The Plan
is to ponder and pray, which
thing leads them to appreciate
the Atonement, and to speedily
repent of their sins. Only then,
will they find the happiness
that has been prepared
for the Saints.

Even when we
are fully committed,
it is our regularly recurring
repentance that will bless us with
repetitive moments of confirmation;
when will be able to say, as did those
in Zarahemla, that through the miracle
of forgiveness, by the power of the
Atonement, our hearts have once
again been changed through
faith on the name of
Jesus Christ.

The
Atonement
of Jesus Christ has
such power that even if we
have been gravely wounded
by our sins, they will not heal
imperfectly, leaving soul scars.
Thru the application of the Balm
of Gilead, the adhesions that
are left behind by telestial
trauma will fade away
until all evidence of
damage has been
erased.

One of the
basic messages
of the Restoration
is that Adam and Eve
fell that they might have
joy while on earth, as well
as in heaven, thru repentance
that had been activated by
their faith in the power
of the Atonement to
save them from
their sins.

Forgiveness
of sins through
repentance is built
upon our understanding
of the Atonement, which is
why it surely formed the basis
of our pre-mortal classroom
curriculum. The initiative is
now ours, to experience
religious recognition,
or the re-knowing
of what we have
beforehand
learned.

The account of the Creation that was written by Moses provided only the details that relate to the Fall of Adam and Eve, and to the Atonement of Christ, which is the doctrine that we must understand in order to have the faith to live abundantly and become heirs of salvation. In the scriptures, The Plan refers to worlds without number, but the application of its principles and doctrines relates only to the sphere upon which we live.

The Holy Ghost prompts us to examine what it means to be anxiously engaged, inspires us to plumb the depths of our commitment to the Savior, sensitizes us to the nobility of His work, expands upon our visions of immortality, personalizes the Atonement, and helps us to retain a remission of our sins and to remain consciously aware of our close proximity to the angels in heaven who wield the sword of justice.

The
Holy Ghost
unshackles us
from the unpleasant
consequences of Justice.
Darkness is the conjoined twin
of misery, but the obedience of faith
frees us to embrace the truth, to make
intelligent choices, to perform purposefully,
to carry on convincingly, and to progress
persistently; in short, to rise above the
cares of the world by becoming
at-one with Christ through
His sacrifice for our
sins.

Those
of us who desire
to obtain forgiveness
have learned that we must
not hold anything back. It will
be necessary to invest everything we
have, and that includes our assurance,
anticipation, confidence, conviction,
expectation, and trust in the power
of the Atonement to deliver on
its almost incomprehensible
promise from our Lord
that He can save us
from our sins.

Because the testimony of Jesus is the spirit of prophecy, the Holy Ghost becomes a facilitator who helps to bring others of God's children to the knowledge of His Plan, to their own independent testimony of the Savior, and to faith in His Atonement, just as He has done with those who are already members of His Church.

Only if we
exhibit the moral
discipline to incorporate
into our behavior the steady
guidance of the Holy Spirit, will
we be able to recognize, address,
reverse, and erase with finality,
the imbalance in our lives.
That direction will lead
us to the Atonement
of Jesus Christ.

The effects
of sin are inevitable
and are inescapable, but
for the intercession, by our
faith, of the Atonement. The
Maker and Fashioner of the
universe must intervene by
engaging laws that restore
equilibrium, or all is lost.
The Holy Ghost exists to
help to restore that
state of balance
in our lives.

We must
drag our broken
and bleeding bodies
to the temple, because it
is there that we will receive
the transfusions of a spiritual
element. It is a heavenly dialysis
center, where worldly contaminants
may be removed from our systems,
because we are simply incapable
of accomplishing the task on
our own. The resources we
need are only found in
the Atonement, that
is taught in the
endowment.

The endowment predisposes us to become all that God is, by incorporating His image and likeness into our own being and nature. For the endowment to fulfil its promises, we must care for the earthly tabernacles of our celestial spirits. It is only in the Atonement that we find a way for our corruptible bodies to become clean and pure, even worthy temples that are full of the light of life.

In
the Spirit
Prison, those who
accept the Fulness
of the Gospel and have
had the necessary ordinances
of exaltation performed in their
behalf in the temple, will be heirs of
the Celestial Kingdom of glory. "These
shall dwell in the presence of God and
his Christ forever and ever." (D&C 76:62).
This is an example of the Atonement of
Christ at its very best. "The presence of
the Lord shall be as the melting fire
that burneth, and as the fire which
causeth the waters to boil."
(D&C 133:41).

Faith is dead, without the accompanying work of repentance that is only made possible by the Atonement. Even great faith lacks the power to save us from the unalterable demands of Justice. In order for Mercy to prevail, God provided us with His Mediator, as well as with another Spokesperson Whom we acknowledge as our Comforter, or the Holy Ghost.

Every
time we cast
ourselves upon
the altar of faith,
gratitude swells in
our hearts as we think
of the infinite Atonement
of the Lord. We examine our
lives through the magnifying
glass of the Spirit to look for
ways to improve. Because of
our repentance, the Savior
becomes the wind beneath
our wings, and we find
ourselves flying higher
than eagles.

There is evidence of the
absolute genius behind the Plan
of God, as it focuses our thoughts on
the Spirit, on our covenants, the Savior,
His Atonement, and the commandments.
That discipline expands the capacity of
our understanding, and allows us to
experience how a Gospel-oriented
life that focuses on principles
can be so much greater than
the sum of its parts.

If we allow ourselves
to become isolated from the
sensitivity to our surroundings
that is nurtured by repentance, we
may become inured to our condition
in a way that leaves us past feeling.
When that is so, then the power of
the Atonement is of no effect in
our lives, and for us, the Savior
of the world suffered in the
Garden of Gethsemane
and died on the Cross
at Calvary, for
naught.

Those
timid souls who
are of weak character
and faltering faith in The
Plan of our Great Creator,
frequently think that they can
side-step both the requirements
of repentance and the demands
of discipleship. But it is because
they have never experienced the
freedom enjoyed by those who
move with willpower and grit
along the strait and narrow
path, due to the liberating
influence generated by
the Atonement of
Jesus Christ.

It was through His supernal demonstration of a magnificent omniscience that our Savior Jesus Christ negotiated with Justice to execute the Law of Mercy. Our Heavenly Father had beforehand conceived the Atonement, in order to bring about our metamorphosis. The sacrifice of the Savior liberates us from condemnation to remain as fallen creations in a cruel twist of fate. We would instead be transformed by the power of heaven into beings of light.

The Atonement is difficult for some to grasp because it was conceived in heaven. It is not of this world, and so if they try to wrap their finite minds around it, they will fail to do so, for it can only be spiritually discerned.

Our salvation has less to do with cherubim and a flaming sword, and more to do with our faith, repentance, baptism, forgiveness mercy, Atonement, the Sacrament, and, ultimately, redemption. Because of these principles, the Law of Mercy trumps the Law of Justice through forgiveness, and all is because of the sacrifice of our Lord and Savior, Jesus Christ.

Even as their
ears are assaulted
by sounding brass and
tinkling cymbals, those with
a strong testimony of repentance
will find within the Atonement of
Christ the ability to sift through the
discordant cacophony of confusing
voices to find rhythms of revealed
truth and a harmonious balance
between heaven and earth that
leads to forgiveness of sin.
Our craving to be clean
finds its expression in
celestial sparks that
ignite our desire
to continually
repent.

When
we have
been born
again thru the
Atonement, our
orientation is more
toward the expansive
laws of the eternal world
than it is to the restrictive
confines that are defined by
our physical surroundings. The
Spirit guides us to the physicality
of heartfelt repentance, and to an
appreciation of the otherworldly
doctrine of the Atonement. The
Plan of God bridges both time
and space, by guiding us to
a condition that is more
one of "becoming" than
it is of simply
"being."

The verbal exchange that takes place at the veil is a rehearsal. It prepares us to be clothed with both immortality and eternal life; to more closely resemble our Father in Heaven in His image and in His likeness. The dialogue that occurs during the endowment suggests that we are gods and goddesses in embryo, and that our genome is divine. It extends the promise that it is our destiny to mature until, in an eternal progression that relies upon the infinite and eternal Atonement of Christ, we will have been molded to go where no-one has ever gone before, and to tread upon the sanctity of space, to walk in the footsteps of the Gods.

Faith is dead, without the accompanying work of repentance that is made possible by the Atonement. Even great faith lacks the power to save us from the unalterable demands of Justice. So that Mercy might prevail, God provided us with a Mediator.

If we hope to
be able to successfully
deal with the inequalities of
life and escape the quicksands
of self-pity, we must personalize
the lessons of the Atonement, and
that is best accomplished during the
hour of prayer that is found within
Sacrament meetings. Pondering the
Savior's forgiveness of our sins, we
visualize Him standing before the
golden gate of heaven, patiently
waiting for us to acknowledge
the transcendent beauty of
His power to transform
our lives.

An
insidious
negative force
can intrude upon
our affairs, and the
Atonement is its only
viable countermeasure.
Its sole stipulations are
that we confess when we
have, in any magnitude,
embraced the opposites
that lie before us, and
that we unhesitantly
undertake the safety
protocols required
by repentance to
bring us back
to our home
in heaven.

The Atonement looks right into the jaws of spiritual death without averting its eyes. At the Council, it was not the Savior, but the Devil who was the first to blink. In consequence of his rebellion against every element of light and truth, he was unceremoniously cast out of heaven, a fallen son of the morning.

The only certifiable fire retardant that can be dumped on the raging inferno of sin is the Atonement. Because of the Savior's sacrifice, we receive the kind of immortal body that we will need ensuing the resurrection, if we hope to dwell in another kind of fire, which is the divine fervor of eternal life.

The Savior of the
world has negotiated with Justice
to purchase our sins with the legally
recognized currency of the Atonement.
His voluntary act of sacrifice is perfectly
balanced and attuned to accomplish the
task at hand, to overcome death and
hell, which are the exact opposites of
eternal life and heavenly glory in
the Celestial Kingdom.

Since
the testimony
of Jesus Christ is
the spirit of prophecy,
the Holy Ghost becomes a
facilitator who helps to bring
others of God's children to the
knowledge of His Plan, to their
own independent witness
of the Savior, and to faith
in His Atonement.

The symbolism of the
Lord's Last Supper has been
beautifully preserved for us in
the scriptures. (See John 13:1-35).
In accordance with revelation, the
ordinance of the Sacrament has been
restored. Broken bread represents the
torn flesh of the Savior, and the water
represents the blood that was shed
during His sacrifice, in the act
of Atonement for our sins.

Baptism
for the remission
of our sins activates
the redemption exemption
that is a codicil to the Law of
Justice. The terms of our lease on
life have been renegotiated to our
everlasting advantage by the Savior.
The intervention of Mercy has been
achieved, but at an unfathomable
cost that rests squarely upon the
strength of His infinite and
eternal Atonement.

When we
walk in the light of
revealed truth, and we
enter into life by way of the
Atonement of Jesus Christ, we
may be pleasantly surprised by
the lavish accommodations that
He has provided in the household
of faith. His forgiveness removes
the awful stains of sin from the
tapestries upon which have been
embroidered the experiences
that embellish our lives.

During the process of our repentance, we follow a natural progression, but the real power that stems from the Atonement and saves us from our sins hinges upon a deeper and more abiding faith. It is "the substance of things hoped for, the evidence of things not seen." (Hebrews 11:1).

Without the
Atonement of Christ,
we would be devoid of the
blessings we receive because of
our obedience to covenants, and
we would remain miserable, living
in a state of separation from the
presence of not only our Father
in Heaven, but also that of His
only begotten Son, as well
as the Holy Ghost.

We persevere
in our obedience to
our covenants, because
we have strong testimonies
that the principles governing
the Fall of Adam, as well as the
Savior's Atonement, were great and
eternal purposes that were prepared
from the foundation of the world.
We trace our obedience back to
our baptisms, that testified of
our desire to participate in
every ordinance of The
Plan of Salvation.

We have
faith that
there is enough
room and enough
time in the eternities
for each of us develop
the capacity to see beyond
the limited horizon of our
vision all the way to the
Atonement of Christ, a
sacrifice that reaches
out to the best of us,
to the worst of us,
and to everyone
in between.

To some
degree, we find
ourselves susceptible
to the influences of the
Seven Deadly Sins. In every
case, however, the Atonement
of Christ stands ready to rescue
us. Repentance rekindles our zest
for life by reviving our enthusiasm,
restoring our divine inspiration, and
by recalibrating the celestial compass
that rests within our beating hearts,
which manifests itself as a burning
feeling within our bosom.

Our Heavenly Father's
Plan has provided us with a
regularly recurring reassurance
of a religious recalibration that auto
corrects with a celestial precision. Faith
envelops us in an intuitive appreciation of
where we came from, the sure knowledge of
why we are here, and the confidence to know
exactly where we are going. It gives us the
courage to maintain forward momentum
during our journey to the Atonement,
so we won't lose our balance,
fall down, and injure, or
mortally wound, our
divine nature.

The account of the Creation that was written by Moses provided only the details that relate to the Fall of Adam and Eve, and to the Atonement of Christ, which is the doctrine that we must understand in order to have the faith to be clean from the blood and sins of our generation, live life in abundance, and become heirs of salvation.

Faith prompts us to examine what it means to be anxiously engaged, inspires us to plumb the depths of our commitment to the Savior, sensitizes us to the nobility of His work, expands upon our visions of immortality, personalizes His Atonement, and stimulates us to remain consciously aware of the promise of eternal life, and of our close proximity to heaven itself.

We have
faith that Jesus
is the Father of our
spiritual regeneration,
and like the parent that we
all want to be, He is there to
heal our infirmities and bind
up our wounds, every time we
stumble and whenever we fall,
because of the weight we have
been attempting to carry by
ourselves. Even though we
may forget all about the
Atonement, the Savior
will never, ever,
forget about
us.

Since there
must be opposition
in all things, even as
there is faith, so must there
be its worldly counterparts. In
our day, the grip of fear paralyzes
many of God's children. Today, more
than ever, we need a hope in Christ. We
need the assurance of peace, that our
lives are moving in the direction
of our dreams, and that the
Atonement can show us
how to lasso the
stars.

When we
look with the
eye of faith thru
a spiritual prism, the
Atonement will touch us
to see beyond the limited
horizon of our sight all the
way to eternity. Through the
power of the Holy Ghost, our
eyes will be opened, that we
might begin to understand
the reach of the Savior's
influence on our
lives.

We are blessed to
enjoy temple worship after
our faith has been religiously
recalibrated thru repentance. It
allows us to become reinvigorated
by the refreshing breeze of celestial
air. The endowment paints a portrait
of free-will where we may take risks.
If, in our efforts, we fail to measure
up to its ordinances, the Savior will
always step in to intervene in our
behalf, by using the bargaining
chip of the Atonement to
placate the demands
of Justice.

It is nothing
less than our faith that
binds together the building
blocks that activate the power
of the Atonement. Without faith,
the fabric of our lives unravels in
a process leading to disintegration.
When the anchor of the knowledge
of the Atonement is missing, our
experiences can be like a train
wreck in slow motion that is
frustratingly repeated
over and over.

Without
knowledge,
there can be no
faith; without faith,
there can be no light,
and without light there
can be no recognition of
religious truth; and without
spiritual enlightenment, when
one of the three elements of
faith, light, and truth is lost,
then all must be forsaken.
Our fortunes rest upon the
basis of how completely
we embrace the power
of the Atonement
of Christ.

When we are infused with the knowledge of God thru the Atonement of our Savior Jesus Christ, our "bodies shall be filled with light, and there shall be no darkness in (us); and that body which is filled with light comprehendeth all things." (D&C 88:67).

We
who have
the faith to
be born again
are set free by the
Atonement of Christ
to reach our potential.
We are as the acorns of
mighty oaks, vitalized by
faith and basking in the
nurturing influence of
God, to grow to the
full stature of
our spirits.

Sooner or later, there will be for each of us who has undergone a spiritual heart transplant a moment in the sun, when the steady light of understanding illuminates our minds so that the divine potential of the new organs audibly beating in our chests might be confirmed by our deep and abiding faith in the capability of Christ's Atonement to sustain the unfolding process of our spiritual healing.

The white-hot sparks of faith that have been struck off the Divine Anvil of God may smolder for a while, before they ignite the flame of our resolve. But when they do, we will have developed the power to do whatsoever thing is right, and that is to throw ourselves on the mercy seat of our Lord and Savior, and to rely upon His Atonement to save us from our sins.

Exalting faith
has the capacity to
be the fundamental fiber
within a glorious tapestry whose
intricate design reveals itself as an
expression of the Savior's Atonement.
When it allows us to attain the full
stature of our spirits because our
nature has finally conformed to
the pattern of heaven itself, our
perfect frames will burst free
of the shackles of our clay,
and express themselves as
astonishingly vibrant
coats of many
colors.

The Atonement of Christ will lead us in the direction of perfection, which means that we persevere to the point that we feel that we have no more to give. It is at the point of utter exhaustion that we must refocus on that power which is greater than ourselves, if we hope to be able to survive the ordeal that God, in His greater wisdom, is asking us to endure.

The
Atonement
allows us to see
beyond the limited
horizon of our sight;
to be touched by a vision
of the virtue of the word of
God. Our faith enables us to
savor revealed truth with a
discriminating taste that
discerns the distinctive
flavor of eternal
worlds.

The Atonement is a powerful financial device that provides over-draft protection as we invest in the theater of life. It stands as a guardian, or a personal asset manager, to make sure that when our foolish debts become due and payable, our checks that have been co-signed by the Savior can only be cashed by a creditor who goes by the name of Justice, but only if they have been previously endorsed by Mercy.

Similar to a
dialysis machine, the
Atonement of Jesus Christ
is a mechanism that removes
impurities from our hearts, so
that we might enjoy the faith
necessary to build the holy
accommodations that are
worthy of the habitation
of our spirits.

The
Atonement
draws upon the
magnificent power
of all three members
of the Godhead, so that
we may become increasingly
receptive to flashes of insight;
to be cast off into streams of
revelation that carry us along
in the quickening currents of
direct experience with our
Heavenly Father, with
Jesus Christ and
with the Holy
Ghost.

When
the octane
rating of the fuel
that fires our faith in
the Atonement of Christ
is too low, we may be able to
just barely get by, but only for a
time. As we limp along with our
engines of discipleship misfiring
badly, the incessant knocking
sound of fear will ultimately
overpower us, until we deny
the faith, and we are no
longer valiant in the
testimony of
Jesus.

The progress we make in life centers on what we do with the Atonement of Jesus Christ and upon what His Gospel does for us. Ideally, they will create a connection of understanding with the ability to bridge the gap that would otherwise exist between heaven and earth.

The
coat of
many colors
was a gift from
Joseph's father. So
too, we have received
the fabric of faith as a
gift from our Father Who is
in Heaven. We can be certain
that He has selected every bolt
of cloth, and has thoughtfully cut
each of them to accommodate the
design He has planned for our lives,
and that its dominant, recurring
pattern is our recognition of
the Atonement of His Only
Begotten Son.

The
Atonement
permits us to
free ourselves
from the mire of
sin, and to cleanse
ourselves in the blood
of Jesus Christ; to stand
steadily upon Gospel sod.
Our faith separates us from
those who precariously hop
about on the flotsam and
the jetsam that bob up
and down, and toss
to and fro, on the
unpredictably
roily sea
of life.

We live in the
midst of Spiritual
Babylon, and recoil as
we encounter a sprawling
wasteland of worldliness that
reeks of the rotting stench of sin.
But we must not allow our faith in
the cleansing power of the Lord's
infinite and eternal Atonement
to be contaminated by the raw
sewage that is unleashed by
Satan's servants, who are
often thinly disguised
as sanitation
workers.

We are
lucky to have
been blessed with
faith in the Atonement
of Christ, and to become
witnesses of His power. We
are sanctified in Him by the
grace of God, and through
the shedding of His blood,
which is in the covenant
of His Father unto the
remission of our sins.
We are consecrated
to become holy
and without
spot.

While
the desire to
obtain gold can
certainly corrupt us,
the bright, shiny metal
that cannot be corroded
symbolizes the purity that
turns our thoughts to the
Atonement of Christ, and
to the Celestial Kingdom,
whose gilded streets will
dazzle our eyes as the
gates of heaven swing
open in an invitation
for each one of us
to enter into the
presence of
the Lord.

The Atonement of Christ encourages an interrelationship between our physical and spiritual well-being and obedience, that must exist if we hope to nurture the faith to obey His divine design during the assembly of our mortal tabernacles that have been envisioned by Him to transform into the holy temples of our spirits.

The
faithful see
the attention and
adoration of the world
for what it is: Nothing more
than a satanic seduction that
can influence us to abandon
our faith in the Atonement
of Christ and leave our
coats of many colors
hanging unattended
and unused in the
backs of our
closets.

It
is in
the House
of the Lord
that we see how
the Atonement can
become infinite and
eternal in its scope. In
the endowment, we learn
the basic math that it is the
legal tender of the Atonement
that is all the currency we will
need, to purchase the golden
tickets that will guarantee
each of us safe passage
back to our home
in heaven.

Faith is more than our intellectual assent. Its influence extends as far as our deeds. Therefore, works that reflect our reliance upon the Atonement of our Savior Jesus Christ become an important companion not only to faith but also to a testimony and conversion.

In every age,
the tender shoots of
young testimony spring up
and are carefully nurtured in
accordance with Alma's inspired
formula, without the ecclesiastical
embroidery that too often needlessly
complicates the simple sewing, and
sowing, of Gospel messages that
focus upon the Atonement
of Jesus Christ.

The
false gods of
secular humanism
and other ideologies
that extoll the virtues of the
intellect and demand tangible
proof will destroy our faith in
the Atonement. They will divert
us from following a Plan whose
successful execution hinges
upon nourishing the seeds
of our innocent faith in
its ability to save us
from our sins.

Our testimony of truth, and in particular of the Atonement, includes these three essential elements. Initially, is our introduction to an eternal principle. Second, is our correct understanding of the Lord's counsel concerning the principle, and finally, is our experience with the principle, which is the fruits of faith. (See Galatians 5:2).

The fabric of our faith in the Atonement of the Savior Jesus Christ is as spiritual swaddling clothes that have been integrated into our coats of many colors. It resonates with intrinsic light that betrays the fact that its vibrancy can be traced to much more than just pigment and dye.

Our faith in the power of the Atonement will lead to purposeful performance. It must involve a vital, personal commitment to a practical belief. But at the end of the day, our good works lack the efficacy for salvation. Faith in the Savior of the world is what activates God's grace in our behalf, and it is that power alone that will save us, after all we can do.

At the Bar
of Justice, the
evidence will be
presented, and our
previous conformity with
or rejection of eternal law
will determine our reward or
punishment. Our innate capacity
to generate faith in the Atonement
makes our trials more than just
a game of chance. In fact, the
cards have been marked and
the deck has been stacked
in our favor.

As imperfect mortals who are struggling to believe what we do not see, the reward of our maturing faith is to see what we believe. Some things just have to be believed to be seen, before our emerging faith in the Atonement has been shaped by our experience, and we can say, as did the believing man who had been blind from his birth, but was healed by the Savior: "One thing I know, whereas I was blind, now I see." (John 9:25).

Our witness of the efficacy of the Atonement of Christ requires the moral element of responsibility that we call faith. Of those to whom much is given, however, much is expected. The gift of faith demands action. Therefore, when we exercise free will, even if we perform good works, without faith, it falls short. It "is dead, being alone." (James 2:17).

During our journey of faith to the Atonement of Jesus Christ, it is necessary to take a few halting steps into the darkness, in order to let the spiritual strong searchlight of truth illuminate the way. Only after the trial of our faith, will it be confirmed by the Spirit that the Savior is both its Author and its Finisher, Who has us covered, both coming and going.

The
Atonement
of Christ gives every
thread in the fabric of
our own faith a vim, vigor,
vitality, and a vivacity that
is unique to holy vestments.
Their steadfast colors will
never fade, save it be thru
neglect or unbelief. They
will remain impervious
to blemishes, but for
the stubborn stains
of unresolved
sin.

During times
of our weakness, it
may seem to us that the
easier way out is to adopt
the ways of the world, and that
it is harder to acknowledge that
there is an autobiographical thread
within each of us that leads all the
way back to heaven. Sometimes, we
can't see the forest for the trees, or
that we are as the acorns of mighty
oaks. Because of our distractions,
we lose focus on the things that
are most important in life, like
the Atonement of our Lord
and Savior Jesus Christ.

If we want
to develop the
faith to choose the
Atonement of Christ, we
must expend soul-sweat. As
Robert Frost mused: "I shall be
telling this with a sigh somewhere
ages and ages hence: Two roads
diverged in a wood, and I took
the one less traveled by, and
that has made all the
difference."

If we allow ourselves
to succumb to our fears,
and permit faithlessness to
handcuff the expression of our
conscious decision to choose the
Savior's Atonement, all that will be
left in the end is a monochromatic
and one-dimensional compromise
that leaves us with a hollow core
of emptiness in the pit of our
stomachs and terror in our
hearts. Faith, for a good
reason, is fear that has
said its prayers.

Those
with faith to
rely on the merits
of Christ and choose
His Atonement are like
"brave Horatius, the Captain
of the Gate," who declared: "To
each of us upon this earth, death
cometh soon or late. And how can
we die better, than facing fearful
odds, for the ashes of our fathers
and the temples of our gods?"
(Thomas Macaulay).

Those who surrender their dreams and deny the power of the Atonement sell their birthright to the lowest bidder for a mess of pottage. Once they have made the exchange, they may far too easily be dragged down to a hell on earth where, with terror, they realize that it is they who have purchased and decorated the prison cell into which they have been cast, with the spurious currency of the deceiver.

The Atonement of Christ
commits us to the arduous process
of choosing the harder right, that is
accompanied by a spiritual rebirth. Its
alternative would leave us to follow a
wobbly course that leads to the easier
wrong. But that is a devilish detour
that is characterized by the desire
to subvert The Plan of God by
forcing the capitulation by
Mercy to the miscarriage
of Justice, wherein we
would somehow be
saved in our
sins.

The difficult decision that was made by Adam and Eve in the Garden to choose the harder right instead of the easier wrong, obviated the 'Progression Paradox' that had faced them, wherein they would have remained forever in "a state of innocence, having no joy, for they knew no misery; doing no good, for they knew no sin." 2 Nephi 2:23). Their choice, however, was anticipated by the Atonement of Jesus Christ.

Through the Atonement of Jesus Christ, we are exposed to a constant flow of insight, intuition, inspiration, and revelation that simply streams forth in a downpour of divine direction. It blesses us as we walk along illuminated pathways, and we exercise our faculties of mind and spirit. The Plan leads us to the community of Christ, so that, together, we may collectively experience the guidance of the Holy Ghost.

If we allow it to do so, the Atonement will charge the air in the theater of life as fire in the sky, with an electricity that represents the inevitable merger of the universal encouragement of the Light of Christ, with the pointed and providential guidance of the Holy Ghost, that is His gift of faith to believe.

Our attempts
to comprehend the
Atonement help us to
understand ourselves. It
is when we have discovered
the answers to where we came
from and why we are here that
we will be prepared to embark,
with unbridled confidence, upon
an incredible journey into our
future, to see with the eye
of faith just where it is
that we are going.

With our faith
to choose the harder
right, while distaining the
easier wrong, we will avoid
the world's amusement parks,
and will gratefully utilize the
aid station of the Atonement
that has been providentially
positioned in Zion. We will
use the Savior's sacrifice
as a celestial barometer
that is calibrated to a
scale that measures
the capacity of
our hearts.

It was Jesus
Christ, under the direction
of our Father in Heaven, Who
created the earth upon which we
stand as a learning laboratory, and
as a telestial testing center. It would
be a citadel of higher education, and a
home where we would be blessed to have
all of the tools that could conceivably
be necessary to validate God's faith
in us; to see if we could muster
an equivalent faith in His Plan
for us, and in the infinite
Atonement of His
Son.

It just
may be the
Atonement that
causes our blood to
run hot, reminiscent of
the microwave background
radiation from the creation of
our universe billions of years ago,
as well as of the fiery cauldron of
experience that was catalyzed in
a garden setting eastward in
Eden, that was not so
very long ago.

When we have stockpiled sufficient assets in our spiritual savings accounts, when they are nearing depletion, or even if our accounts are overdrawn, the financial institution whose reserves are found within the Atonement dispenses pennies from heaven, which is the currency of faith in its myriad forms.

When
we encounter
the true doctrine of
the Atonement of Jesus
Christ, our sinews resonate
with recognition. In this way,
every one has been blessed with
the innate capacity to hearken to
the voice of the Spirit, even the
Holy Ghost, that one day they
might return to the warm
embrace of their Father
Who waits for them
in heaven.

The
Atonement
blesses us with a
pure form of focus,
that transforms our five
natural senses into something
wonderful, by a heaven-sent sixth
sense that defies description. Physical
and spiritual resources work in tandem
to compound each other, and to condition
us through the patience of faith, the miracle
of repentance, the diligence of baptism, the
sweet spirit of the Holy Ghost, and our
soul-sustaining renewal in the
Sacrament of the Lord's
Supper.

Wo unto
those who only
casually receive the
illumination of faith
that is a blessing of the
Atonement and that has been
so freely given. Because of their
misguided obsession with temporal
trivia, they carelessly fritter away
their faith, and waste the days of
their probation rooting through
telestial trash in a fruitless
effort to find meaning in
the barren dumpsters
of their empty
lives.

By allowing
ourselves to be
habitually distracted
by trifling concerns until
they become the center of our
attention and even our obsession,
we ignore our innate yearning to
exercise faith in the Atonement
of Jesus Christ, and thereby
we commit a grievous
sin of omission.

Those who are lazy in their Gospel discipleship might ask: "What do I want out of life?" while those of faith inquire: "What would God have me do?" At a basic level, idleness is the devil's workshop, and so our refusal to be up and doing in the wake of the atonement of Jesus Christ is sin. It is wasting our precious opportunities for renewal in fruitless pursuits, when we should have been engaged in other and better activities for which we have been blessed with God-given capabilities.

Society pays
a heavy price when it
lacks a faithful focus on
the Atonement of Jesus Christ.
For example, when its spiritual
equilibrium has become disoriented
and its moral compass is spinning out
of control, its values are quickly adjusted
in an unconscious attempt that is misguided
and vain, to regain a state of balance
between heaven and earth.

An unprincipled and faithless society deals with its spiritual myopia with a knee-jerk reaction that simply ratchets down its expectations. In the end, a culture that lacks the fire of faith in the Atonement of Jesus Christ will demand very little of its members, and will receive from them in kind.

In a
wasted attempt
to avoid cultural
implosion, and for
the sake of collective
expediency, the target has
been moved so many times
to score repetitive bulls-eyes,
that no-one seems to be able
to concede that it is the arrow
of faith that has strayed far
from the mark, which is
the Atonement of
Christ.

We lose
our focus and
our faith gradually,
just as we lose the acuity
of our vision over time. Whether
it is the letter of the law to rely
upon the Atonement of Christ, or
an eye chart that is beyond our
comprehension, we are legally
blind. Although we have eyes,
we cannot see what has
been clearly placed
before us.

Repentance concentrates on available resources, and by using the power of Atonement, it harnesses them. It converts our substance into an energy, whereby positive, substantial, and significant change can take place. Those who decline the offer of the riches of eternity that have been unfolded to their view by the Savior's sacrifice, are doomed to live their lives in scarcity of their spiritual needs.

If we no
longer believe
that the Atonement of
Jesus Christ has the power
to save us from our sins, the
compromise of our conversion can
often be attributed to a lack of faithful
focus that initiated a flat spin from which
we were unable to recover. The blame for the
demolition of our discipleship, as well as the
chain-reaction of unfortunate consequences
that follows, may be laid at the doorstep of
others, but at the end of the day, it comes
down to us, and to no-one else. The
Spirit may guide us, but we are the
architects of our own fate.
(See Philippians 2:12).

The faithful find mentors whom they can emulate, instead of scapegoats that are easy to blame. Instead of looking for easier answers, they dig deeply to uncover healthier solutions thru the Atonement to the problem of sin that we all face.

Our best intentions relating to how we use the Atonement may be noble, but vision without work is dreamery, and even if we work hard, without vision, we are doomed to drudgery. If we focus our faith, however, and make the Atonement a vital part of our vision, it will be our destiny to soar with eagles, rather than walk with turkeys.

Paul exhorted the Philippian Saints to work out their own salvation with fear and trembling. He knew that if they put their hearts and their souls into the effort to understand the Atonement, it would leave them physically and spiritually exhausted. Still, he invited them to join him, as he pressed "toward the mark, for the prize of the high calling of God in Christ Jesus." (Philippians 3:14).

When
our focus is
on the Atonement,
we don't get in the thick
of thin things. We cultivate
an equilibrium that is centered
far from the madding crowd, at a
safe distance from the ego-filled
minds of mediocre men. We are
insulated from the tumult, the
confusion, and the cares of
the world, and enjoy an
unshakable firmness
in our faith.

The Atonement protects
us from a false sense of carnal
security, as well as from indifferent
complacency. We view our weaknesses
in positively constructive ways, and are
grateful for our conscious awareness of
opportunities for personal improvement,
and for the tools that we have been
given to accomplish our mortal
mission assignments.

We know that
weaknesses are a
part of the tapestry that
has been woven by God to be
the fabric of our lives. We simply
turn to the inventory of thread that
He has provided within the Atonement,
that enables us to weave imaginative
new patterns that are reflections of
the celebration of our faith in our
Savior's ability to redeem us
from our sins.

The
sacrifice that
was made by the
Savior in the Garden
of Gethsemane pushes us
beyond our normal capacity,
and it instills within us a quiet
resolve to lengthen our stride. To
avoid the fate of those who would
greet the Atonement of Christ with
skepticism, and to insure that our
faith will be animated by energy,
so that we will have no regrets
as we move along our own Via
Dolorosa, we have been given
not only the Light of Christ
but also the gift of the
Holy Ghost.

It is only
thru the sacrifice
of Jesus Christ that we
are able to increase our
metaphysical metabolism,
to burn away as much of the
fat of faithlessness as we can
when our hearts are broken in
the fiery crucible of contrition.
We remain unable, ourselves, to
remove the stain of sin, for just
as long as we remain incapable
of maintaining our unequivocal
subservience to the celestially
crafted doctrine that we call
the Atonement. This we do
in remembrance of Him
Who gave His life
for us.

Obstacles are
frightful demons
that threaten us when
we take our minds off the
Atonement. They loom large
with gratuitous significance. Our
faith endows us with the vision to
see beyond these potential stumbling
blocks. If we turn them into stepping
stones that pave the way to our higher
achievement, it is because we have
been empowered by the capacity
of the Atonement that is an
expansive and creative
engine for positive
change.

Sooner
or later, each of us
must undertake a journey
that will lead to the feet of
the Savior and to His Atonement.
As we move along the Yellow Brick
Road thru the forest of faith toward
the Emerald City of Oz, we use the
brains we have been given to give
our hearts courage, remembering
that the woods would be very
quiet if no birds sang but
those that sang best.

When the
Atonement of Jesus
Christ has re-introduced
us to those noble principles
that guided us throughout our
spiritual kindergarten years in
the pre-earth existence, we are
blessed with the focus of faith
to accompany us during our
return to that more natural
state of harmony with
the heavens.

The celestial
compass that is the
Atonement is calibrated
to be oriented toward truth,
and is always available to guide
the faithful to a safe haven. It is also
there for those who have lost their way,
to bring them into the fold of the Good
Shepherd, and to show others how they
might return to the sanctuary and
security of the community of
Christ from which they
may have strayed.

Those without a
deep and abiding faith in the
Atonement of Jesus Christ lack
spiritual horsepower. Their dearth of
traction is awkwardly apparent, while
their inability to generate spontaneity
is palpable, and their lack of energy
to engage enthusiasm is noticeable.
Their incapacity to spark vitality
is evident, and their failure to
candidly acknowledge the
dynamic relationship that
can exist between God
and themselves is
undisputed.

When a faithless society is weighed in the balances and is found wanting, it can all be traced back to its spiritual bankruptcy on an institutional scale; simply to its denial of the power of the Atonement of Christ. Its motto seems to be: 'Eat, drink, and be merry, for tomorrow we will will surely die.'

Sooner or later, each of us must discover for ourselves that a line has been drawn in the sand. If we then act upon the promptings of the Holy Ghost to seize the power of the Atonement, we will generate a positive energy that will move us forward in the direction of our dreams. Those who have faith to rely upon the merits of Christ thru His sacrifice will cross that line to be saved in the kingdom of God.

We receive no witness until after the trial of our faith. Having said that, those with little or no faith will characteristically throw up defensive dross that is designed to deflect, disrespect, disregard, discourage, or even disparage the power of the Atonement. Such as they may be enthusiastic, but they are still ignorant.

How we generate the faith to believe in the Atonement will either deify or destroy us. Our response to the Savior's entreaties to come unto Him will delineate our dreams, and define our destiny. It will determine how, where and with whom we will spend all eternity. We can almost hear the voice of the Lord as it exclaims: 'Carpe diem!'

There will come
for each of us a great
and dreadful day, when we
will be asked to stand and give
our sworn deposition before God,
angels, and witnesses. On the issue of
faith in the power of the Atonement of
Christ, depending upon our statement, we
will be counted among the sheep or the
goats, and find ourselves on His right
hand, or on His left hand. We should
begin thinking about how we will
respond to the gentle inquiry:
"What think ye of Christ?"

The
Atonement
reminds us of
the suffering of
Jesus in the Garden
of Gethsemane, when it
stimulates our soul-sweat.
It works on our sense of
duty, on our conscience,
and on our scruples, to
persistently prompts us
to act on our faith.
Not our will, but
that of God
shall be
done.

The
Atonement
provides a shield
of protection against
the corrosive spatter of
perspiration cast off by the
destroyer, who pervasively and
persistently is working overtime to
damage our doctrinal defenses, dull
our spiritual sensitivities, diminish
our charitable capacity, deplete
our bounteous reservoirs of
sympathy, and destroy
our devotions.

One of the blessings flowing from the Atonement of Christ is the constant stream of inspiration and revelation that cascades down from above. This insures that we walk along illuminated pathways leading to the only institution that may legitimately claim revelation from divine guidance, and that has received His approbation.

The Atonement of Jesus Christ is the great equalizer. It matters not in what exclusive ecclesiastical country club we may hold a membership, or upon what narrow theological terrace we may have paused to catch our breath. We all need to be up and moving, to come unto Christ.

It is our faith in the Atonement that teaches us to always face the Son, that we might feel the warmth of its rays upon our cheeks, listen with greater sensitivity to hear the word of the Lord without ambiguity, and see with a lucidity that encourages us to be benevolently blind when we witness the shortcomings of others of our fellow travelers.

The Atonement of Christ
makes it easier to have lips
that have learned to articulate
only positive expressions and that
never speak guile, and shoulders
that have developed the strength
to bear the burdens of those who
have been battered and bruised
by the vicissitudes of life and
who may be faltering under
the heavy burden of sorrow
for unresolved sin.

Our growth now and in eternity hinges largely upon what do we do with the Atonement, as well as upon what the Atonement does for us. Simply stated, it is the Atonement, and our repentance, that establish order in the cosmos, to permit us to progress.

Oliver Wendell Holmes said: "Once a mind has been stretched by a new idea it can never return to its original dimension." Because of the Atonement, we view our afflictions, trials, and tribulations in a new light. We determine to discover for ourselves how the Savior's suffering in Gethsemane was not in vain, but was for our salvation. We resolve to embark upon a ministry of reconciliation with both heaven and earth. (See 2 Corinthians 5:18).

Guidance from above that
comes to us in the forms of spiritual
promptings and subtle impressions are more
common that many would suspect. There are
powerful intuitive communicators that strongly
influence nearly all of us to push forward in
the direction of our dreams, toward a faith
to believe that blesses us with a greater
appreciation of the Atonement
of Jesus Christ.

If we ever hope to venture forth out of the shadow of sin, we must rely upon the guidance that we receive from the Light of Christ and the ministering of angels. If we want to experience the special familiarity that the faithful enjoy with the Savior of the world, we must come unto Christ, through His Atonement.

The
Atonement of
Christ makes it
easier to have backs
that have become sturdy
enough to brace us against
the fierce winds of adversity
and the wiles of the adversary,
and hearts that are receptacles
of pure and virtuous principles
from which we may draw
strength in times
of need.

Pride is motivated
by our own will, while the
Atonement inspires us to seek
to know the will of God. Pride
is driven by the fear of man, while
repentance is nurtured by our love of
the Savior. The applause of the world
rings in the ears of the prideful, but
it is the accolades of heaven that
we hear, that warm our hearts
as our faith convicts us of
our sins. On our journey,
the Spirit accompanies
us as we are brought
down low unto
repentance.

The arrogant, boastful, haughty, and self-centered behavior of the proud is easily outmaneuvered by the deferential, altruistic, modest, and self-effacing nature of those who are quick to repent, whose firm grasp on the Atonement of Christ confirms their faith in God's power to save them from their sins.

In contrast to
the repentant faithful,
who rely upon the merits
of Christ thru His Atonement,
the proud are more comfortable
with their own perception of truth
than they are with His omniscience.
They pit their own abilities against
His mighty priesthood power, their
stubborn will against His gentle
counsel, and their own paltry
overtures against His
mighty works.

Unlike the repentant who rely upon the Atonement, the prideful seek after signs. Because they are past feeling, they require greater and greater intensities of stimulation to entertain the same degree of telestial or theological gratification. What they have received is never sufficient to satisfy their adulterous cravings.

Even
if we hit
a new low after
we have committed
awful sins, if we repent
and trust in the awesome
ability of the Atonement to
bind up and heal our wounds,
we may be long suffering but
not falter in our faith. When
things seem that they could
be no worse, we are at our
best, because then we are
particularly sensitive to
the comfort that comes
thru the whisperings
of the Spirit.

The Atonement
empowers our hands
to lift those who need
our support. It galvanizes
our courage to let our feet
take us to those who have been
imprisoned by poor choices or by
bad habits, or who are hobbled
by ruinous circumstances
that may or may not
have been of their
own doing.

As we determine to repent, as we rely upon the power of the Atonement, we can learn to be humble by receiving chastisement and counsel, by being forgiving those who have offended us, by our service, and by being good examples that teach others to follow the pattern that our Savior has established in His ministry.

If we
ignore the
twin influences
of the Light of Christ
and the Holy Ghost that
nurture our innate yearning to
abhor mischief, but instead allow
ourselves to be habitually distracted
by trifling concerns, we sin by omission
and risk settling for life in a marshland
of mediocrity that quickly degenerates in
to a quicksand of sin, from which there
is no escape unless we take advantage
of the buoyancy that is provided by
the Atonement of Jesus Christ.

The Atonement tests the mettle of our sincerity and our candor with ourselves. It is through repentance that we put our money on the Savior. But we have no proof until we act on the basis of trust. Then, comes the confirmation of the reality as feelings of self-confidence grow and purposeful actions replace tentative overtures. We are all in; we let go and let God.

Timid souls who are cautiously hesitant and tentatively faithful don't consciously intend to lose the desire to repent. Our faith in the power of the Atonement simply fades away, like the slow leak in an automobile tire, and not as a blowout. But, it may often be traced back to the tendency to mischief that may have taken root during a time period of particularly intense vulnerability to the wiles of the Devil.

No
wind can
blow except
it fills our sails to
carry each of us ever
closer to our destination,
without delay or interruption,
and without unnecessary cost,
loss, or sacrifice. All that is
required is a contrite spirit
as we rely upon the power
of the Atonement's steady
breeze, to nudge our
craft onward, as He
lulls our broken
hearts.

Alma taught that, in the absence of repentance for their sins, and without the benefit of covenants, Adam and Eve would have ultimately been miserable. To be certain, they would have lived forever, but without the Atonement, it would have been in an unrelenting state of alienation from the presence of God.

There is nothing
that can make up for
the revelatory rewards that
are such prominent features of
the Gospel. Cheap thrills will never
replace its originality. Neither novelty
nor spectacle can defeat, but can only
delay, implementation of its principles.
The universal influence of the Light of
Christ encourages us to set our sights
on the brightly burning beacon of the
the House of the Lord, as well as of
the Holy Ghost, Who is waiting to
guide us, in the company of the
Atonement, across the ocean
of light to a new world
that awaits our
discovery.

Without redemption from sin, if they were to have partaken of the fruit of the Tree of Life, which is eternal life, or the highest expression of the love of God, it would not have been possible for Adam and Eve to sustain a celestial existence, inasmuch as in their current condition they would have been incapable of obedience to the laws that govern those who merit heavenly glory. Without the Atonement of Jesus Christ, The Plan of Salvation would have been frustrated, not only for them, but also for all of the children of God who would follow after them.

Joseph's coat of many colors can be a metaphor of our faith in the Atonement of Jesus Christ. When we look closely at its fabric, it will teach us that even the most menacing clouds have silver linings, and we will realize that the bright dawning of a new day will follow on the heels of even the darkest of nights.

The Day
of Judgment
does not lie over a
distant horizon, but is
today. We speak, think, and
act according to the celestial,
terrestrial, or telestial laws that
are before us. Just as a barometer
is used to measure the direction in
which the weather is headed, the
Atonement of Jesus Christ helps
us to be continually aware of
the bearing we must follow
if we hope to regain the
shelter of our home
in heaven.

When
Adam and
Eve were driven
from the Garden,
they were "punished"
with the very thing that
would later prove to bring
them the greatest happiness. As
the Sufi poet Rumi observed, our
wounds become portals that allow
light to enter us. A Savior would be
provided for them, but in the interim,
cherubim and a flaming sword were
placed to keep the way of the Tree
of Life, to honor the doctrines of
Justice and Mercy, as well as the
principle of repentance that is
founded on the doctrine of
Atonement. They had been
taught to have faith in
these things after their
fall from grace, in
the Garden.

The truth be
told, it is only when we
have enrolled in the graduate
school of hard knocks, and have
pre-paid the required tuition, that
we obtain the credits that are to be
earned by our strict obedience to the
challenging curriculum of contrition.
We learn to forgive others as Jesus
Christ will forgive each of us our
trespasses, through His infinite
and eternal Atonement for
the sins of the world,
from the beginning
to the end of
time.

Our
acceptance of the
absolute necessity of
the doctrine of opposition
does not give us license to
act recklessly or capitulate in
our behavior to the dark side, in
the mistaken belief that we will be
able to shift the blame and avoid
responsibility for our actions. The
Atonement stands at attention, to
replace the shattered pieces of
our lives, and restore us to
our perfect and proper
frames, so that we
will be as good
as new.

Those
vacillating souls
of weak will who give
up their freedom to choose in
exchange for the flavor of the day,
or for whatever provocative pleasures
their poor choices may provide, will be
snared by Satan and bound by his strong
chains. Too late, they realize that it is their
misguided loyalties that have significantly
curtailed their ability to take advantage
of the Atonement of Jesus Christ to
enjoy the perfect law of liberty.

Habitual sin is a quicksand that mires the unwary in a monotonously repetitive and mind-numbing conformity, as well as in an underwhelming convention. These are the polar opposites of the imaginative spontaneity and the refreshingly distinctive artistic individuality that are among the many blessings that we receive because of our faith in the Savior's Atonement.

The cataracts that are created by our concessions to sin cloud our vision. Our narrow perspective forces us into making comfortless compromises, leaving the landscapes of our lives as nothing more than empty shells. If we do not take advantage of the therapy of repentance thru the Atonement of Jesus Christ, the prognosis is poor for eyes that have lost the ability to see clearly, and that can no longer make the distinctions between good and evil, between light and darkness, between pleasure and pain, and between virtue and vice.

We know by taking a
count of the casualties from
the ideological War in Heaven,
that some of our Father's children
forfeit their privilege to obtain a body.
For those who remained faithful, however,
there came humbling liabilities, for The
Plan required the Creator to die for
our sins to mercifully satisfy the
demands of Justice, in an act
of Atonement that would be
conditional only upon
our repentance.

Our Father in Heaven knows we have the capacity to develop His nature. After all, we are His children. As any reasonable parent would, He simply asks us to obey His household rules. He commands us to repent, to be baptized, and to have faith in the power of the Atonement to save us from our sins. He gives us the gift of the Holy Ghost to help us meet these requirements, so that we might have a hope in our Savior, that we might one day gain readmittance to our family's kingdom of glory.

The
Atonement
puts the day to
day elements of The
Plan in perspective, that
we might more clearly be
able to distinguish the grey
-toned obstacles that lie in
our path. These barriers to our
progression will then stand out
in sharp contrast against the
polychromatic backdrop of
the design that God has
created through the
sacrifice of our
Savior, Jesus
Christ.

To appreciate
just how thoughtfully
the principle of repentance
was conceived, we need to take
ourselves back to the inventive period
when matter was organized, the elements
were brought out of chaos into harmony,
and a Garden was created eastward in
Eden. All was brought to a head when
a Savior was provided, with power to
nullify the transgression of Adam
and Eve, through an Atonement
for their sins as well as for
those of the children of
God who would follow
in their footsteps.

It is nothing
short of sin that
motivates us to drag
our battered and beaten
bodies to a gym that goes
by the name of The Church of
Jesus Christ of Latter-day Saints.
It is there, under the guidance and
direction of priesthood fitness trainers,
that we are invited to participate in the
robust spiritual workout that introduces
us to its most prominent feature, which
is the Atonement of Jesus Christ.

The
Atonement
nurtures our
eternal focus of
faith, permitting us to
"discard the poor lenses
of our bodies, and peer thru
the telescope of truth into the
infinite reaches of immortality."
(Helen Keller). But if we turn our
backs on the invitation to have a
relationship with God through the
Atonement, and remain alienated
from Him by our spiritual death,
it is a foregone conclusion that
we must ultimately surrender
our fortunes to inclinations
that are carnal, sensual,
and devilish.

The
raw and ugly
contamination of sin
is incompatible with the
uncompromising standard of
spiritual hygiene that is required
of those who, one day, through the
Atonement of Jesus Christ, hope to be
restored to their perfect and proper
frames, and to inhabit heaven, to
mingle with the Saints in the
company of God and
His angels.

Wresting the holy scriptures, and suggesting that we are saved by our own works, twists holy writ from its true or proper signification, and perverts it from its correct or rightful application. Lest we deceive ourselves, let it be known that we all need the Atonement, if we wish to be exalted in the Kingdom of God.

Thank God
for the doctrine of
Atonement that helps us
to get thru each day, and
comforts us during every
long night of darkness,
throughout our lives.
Truly, He will stay up
late, and leaves a
light burning for
us, to guide
us back
Home.

The infinite
Atonement of Christ
reestablishes synchronicity
with the divine design of our
Heavenly Father. It conforms to
His majestic clockwork that was
calibrated at the creation of
the world to coordinate
with the time frame
of the heavens.

We try to be perfect
in our repentance, that
God might give us the spirit
of wisdom and of revelation,
to enlighten our understanding,
that we might embrace the hope of
the high calling of our Savior. Because
of His Atonement, we envision chariots of
fire carrying us to heaven, to commune with
angelic beings, the general assembly, and
with the church of the Firstborn.
(See D&C 107:19).

Because of
the Atonement of
Christ, we may remember
our transgressions only in
the sense that they increase
our testimonies. Because there
must needs be opposition in all
things, our Father in Heaven uses
sin, and repentance, to strengthen
us to be more stalwart soldiers
in the army of Christ. In this
way, even our disobedience
ultimately works to our
benefit, as well as to
His advantage.

The road
to our repentance
winds its way thru the
Atonement, and may be
difficult to negotiate, but
it brings about lasting change.
It requires great courage, much
strength, many tears, unceasing
prayers, and untiring efforts.
The work is challenging, but
its retirement benefits are
out of this world.

As soon as
we have mustered
enough courage to
choose the Atonement
of Jesus Christ, we will
be consumed by a divine
fire. After all the elements
of our moral fiber have been
thereby kindled, we will be
aflame with faith, and be
better prepared to face
and to conquer our
worst demons.

The
Atonement
allows us to make
mistakes, to learn from
them, and then to grasp the
horns of sanctuary so that at
the end of the day we may be
justified by the Spirit of God. It
is only with repentance because of
the Atonement, that our homes can
become the wonderful centers for
the talented and gifted that had
been envisioned by our Father
in Heaven before the earth
fell into existence.

It is because
of the Atonement of
Christ that forgiveness can
be liberally applied as a balm
to repair our bruised egos, bitter
feelings, and battered birthrights.
The Savior's example also helps us
to have bowels that are moved to
compassion for others of God's
children who may be struggling
with their own misfortunes, or
who are staggering under
the weight of their own
unresolved sin.

The Devil's bribery
stands in sharp contrast
to the blessings that follow
our repentance. The Atonement
of Jesus Christ is the only weapon
in our arsenal that we will need
to vanquish the father of lies.
Our understanding of Gospel
principles will re-enthrone
the Savior as the God
of this earth.

Our faith, together
with its conjoined twin
of repentance, motivates us
to action by jarring us out of
our complacency regarding the
Atonement. It is there that we
are endowed with the power to
reach out and touch the face
of God with an incorruptible
and unimpeachable spiritual
sixth sense that finds its
expression deep inside
us, even within our
own hearts.

We throw ourselves upon an altar of faith, whose foundation is buttressed by the supernal display of a divine direction that leads us to the Atonement of Christ. It relentlessly drives us forward with unwavering confidence that is inspired by the Holy Ghost. We know that God's power to save will be unleashed in our behalf, to flow over our wounds as a healing balm.

Both free will and
opposition are ever before
us, and the Atonement stands
as a sacred sentinel, beckoning us
to enter in at heaven's gate, to find
the Rest of God. The opposite of the
path that leads to Calvary is the road
to self-indulgence; the opposite of
submission to the will of God is
our self-gratification, and the
opposite of Atonement is
idolatry. It is really
that plain and
simple.

It can be challenging to muster such faith in the Atonement that we are led to the strait and narrow gate of baptism. In fact, "few there be that find it." (Matthew 7:14). We persist in our efforts because we know that the Lord's spiritual fitness program was designed to help us achieve symmetry through repentance. Without it, our day-to-day life would have little stability and would lack coherence.

The Atonement recognizes that even the righteous do not become perfect overnight. Therefore, the Lord has promised that as often as we repent, He will forgive us our trespasses. He will give us enough rope to either hang ourselves, or to lasso the stars and hitch our wagons to eternity. The choice is ours to make.

We are
converted
to the doctrine
of Atonement when
we begin to hear it, as
it calls to us, inviting us
to come in out of the cold;
out of darkness into the light
of day. We are the acorns of
a mighty oak. Our testimony
of Jesus Christ inspires us
to reconnect with our
intrinsic nobility.

It is with a great
deal of empathy that the Holy
Ghost shares our perspective, but
He also sees thru the clarifying and
purifying lens of eternity. He blesses
our lives in many ways by nurturing our
understanding of the Atonement of Christ.
The veil that has been drawn before our
eyes only prevents us, for a moment,
from seeing eternity from His
unobstructed viewpoint.

We can be fully converted to the Atonement and still have very special moments of reconfirmation. The Spirit sometimes works so powerfully upon us that we can say that our hearts have been changed through faith on the name of Christ, that we have been born of Him, and that we have become His sons and daughters. We no longer have the disposition to do evil, but to do good continually.

Faith, light, and truth may be recognized as irreducible common denominators. They are the essential elements of an equation that describes the foundation upon which the Atonement is based. "One for all and all for one!" was the motto of the Three Musketeers. Without faith, light, and truth, said Joseph Smith, we would "degenerate from God, descend to the devil, and lose knowledge," and without without it, we cannot be saved.

The
Holy Ghost
is our mentor and
our teacher. If we are
good students, and have
done our homework, He will
reward us with an illumination
of the doctrine of the Atonement
that will bathe our minds and our
spirits in a cascading current of
insight, intuition, inspiration
and revelation. He will give
us the answer key to the
exam that will follow
shortly on the heels
of our curriculum
in mortality.

A veil has been
drawn across our minds.
But we have the doctrine of the
Atonement, and the unimpeachable
witness of the Holy Ghost, to assist us
in our efforts to probe that mysterious
curtain. In the interim, many of us are
swayed by Satan's siren song, drawn to
the duplicitous shoals of his spiritual
instability, thereon to founder, and
to be pulled under by the riptides
of religious relativism and the
undertow of agnosticism, or
faithless skepticism.

Without
the Atonement, our
society will remain on a
course of self-destruction.
As we learn from D&C 1:16, it
seeks "not the Lord to establish
his righteousness, but every man
walketh in his own way and after
the image of his own god, whose
image is in the likeness of the
world, and whose substance is
that of an idol which waxeth
old and shall perish in
Babylon, even Babylon
the great, which
shall fall."

When we walk in
the light of life and
we go out of our way to
grasp the principles of truth,
we brim over with gratitude as
we discover how our Redeemer has
provided luxurious accommodations
for us in the household of faith by
assigning us a room that has an
unobstructed view of the
Atonement of Christ.

In the grand
scheme of things, it
will make no difference
if we turn to the right or to
the left, because the Atonement
will always be there. When we lift
our eyes to the heavens, the Savior
will be watching us from above. No
matter that we bear the weight of
sin or sorrow with downcast eyes;
He is always beneath us, to lift
us up and carry our burdens.
If we ask in faith, He will
bless us in kind, and
beyond measure.

Because of the Atonement, we are more trusting of others, and we speak without guile. We are more transparent, and we are less prejudicial. We have fewer pretensions, but are more genuine. We are less prone to rationalization, and quicker to forgive. We are grounded in many ways that bestow upon us a reassurance that others cannot know.

Those who
decline the invitation
of the Atonement will often
strangle themselves with material
trinkets and with telestial baubles whose
opacity only obstructs their ability to see
how God has so thoughtfully laid out
before them the smorgasbord of life,
and has charitably invited them to
freely partake of its deights
through repentance.

The Atonement of the Savior puts us in accord with our Father in Heaven, and with the Holy Ghost, Who touch our lives in ways that are sacramental in nature and in their effect on our future. As we ponder the sacrifice of Jesus Christ, we comprehend the truth that we can become beings of light, even as we learn from our experiences during mortality.

The doctrine of
the Atonement provides
us with currency sufficient
for our needs, but it also allows
us, if we so choose, to substitute its
legal tender for wads of counterfeit
cash with which late payments may be
made with both interest and penalties
tacked on for bad behavior. It might
even be that our lease on life would
be threatened with cancellation for
nonpayment of the charges and
levies that accumulate as we
conduct our lives in the
circus of commerce.

The Atonement of Jesus Christ blesses us to comprehend a celestial vernacular that is soothing to our ears and calming to our souls. The voice of the Spirit can be rhythmical and melodious. As we hear it quietly whisper: "You're a stranger here," it is comforting for us to realize that we "have wandered from a more exalted sphere."
(Eliza R. Snow).

Faith in
the Atonement of
Christ creates a bridge
of understanding between
the secular and the divine.
Life, with all its twists and
turns, and its permutations
and combinations, suddenly
makes sense, as we begin
to understand the mind
and the will of our
Father in Heaven.

We marvel
at the intricacies of
the Atonement, and wonder,
as did Paul: "O the depth of the
riches both of the wisdom and the
knowledge of God! How unsearchable
are his judgments, and his ways past
finding out! For who hath known
the mind of the Lord? Or who
hath been his counsellor?"
(Romans 11:33-34).

As we consider
the elements of The
Atonement, it seems that
our faith should remain fixed
on the revelations the Lord has
given us that relate to our world,
and not on mysteries that have not
been revealed to us, may never be
revealed, or that just may not
be pertinent to our current
circumstances.

Sooner or later, we must all make our way to Christ by way of the Atonement, as did those during the reign of King Josiah, who" went up into the house of the Lord, and all the men of Judah and all the inhabitants of Jerusalem with him, and the priests, and the prophets, and all the people, both small and great. And (they) made a covenant before the Lord, to walk after the Lord, and to keep his commandments and his testimonies and his statutes with all their heart and all their soul, (and) to perform the words of the covenant. And all the people stood to the covenant." (2 Kings 23:2-3).

Willing participants
in life's Three Act Play are
now and forever independent in
that stage of development to which
their decisions have led them. Poised
at the edge of forever, they need little
incentive other than the Atonement of
Christ to cast themselves off into the
unknown possibilities of existence,
to boldly go where none but the
faithful have gone before.

The Atonement petitions the court for a summary dismissal of all charges that have been lodged against us. Trial proceedings have already been docketed to follow the conclusion of our mortal experience. To avoid a reversal of our fortunes, we must pay our Advocate the retainer of a broken heart and contrite spirit, for He is even now prepared to plead our case in advance of the commencement of that heavenly tribunal.

When cultural
collapse is imminent,
external controls are often
imposed to manipulate behavior;
to maintain at least a semblance
of societal steadiness. Our escalating
dependence on laws to regulate moral
discipline and to conform our conduct
to something that at least resembles
integrity says something about us,
and about our critical need for
the Atonement of Christ to
step in and provide
stability in our
lives.

As the seasons of our lives unfold before us, we realize how much we need the influence of the Atonement as we engage The Plan of Salvation. "For life is a sheet of paper white, where each of us may write a line or two, and then comes night. Greatly begin! If thou hast time for but a line, make that sublime. Not failure, but low aim, is crime." (James Lowell).

When we
are given the
gift of the Atonement,
we often leave it untouched
and undisturbed in its original
packaging. We forget that the Savior
will always be there to help us make
important choices and keep our
promises, as we engage the
principles of The Plan
of Salvation.

One of the
terrible consequences
of the fascination of Babylon
with telestial titillation, and with
its fixation on the vain and trifling
images of the world, is its insensitivity
to spiritual impressions and whisperings
that it might have received had it been
even remotely interested in learning
more about the eternity-altering
ramifications of the Savior's
Atonement.

The Lord selects those
who are humble and worthy,
and then He tutors them through
the power of the Holy Ghost and the
influence of the Atonement, revealing
His will unto them. Those whom He selects
are "the weak things of the world." (D&C 1:19).
As President Kimball once stated: "Christianity
did not go from Rome to Galilee. It was
the other way around. In our day, the
routing is from Palmyra to Paris,
and not the reverse."

A tenet of faith of The Church of Jesus Christ of Latter-day Saints is that its members believe that The Plan of God provides us with institutional and personal continuing revelation that comes from Heavenly Father through the medium of the Holy Ghost. This power is intimately related to our appreciation of the ability of the Atonement to engage Justice, to bring to pass Mercy. However, "looking for the spectacular, we often miss the constant flow of revealed communication that comes."
(Spencer W. Kimball).

Blind opposition,
enmity, hatred, hostility,
obstinacy, and intolerance
are the raw manifestations of
pride, but these are overwhelmed
by the accommodation, charity,
faith, approachability, hope,
and sociability of those
who rely upon the
Atonement.

The Atonement of Christ purifies us from caustic influences, and decontaminates us from the toxicity that is so prevalent in the world. It neutralizes the homogenization process that can occur as we are tossed about by the vagaries and vicissitudes of life.

The Plan
teaches that
darkness cannot
abide the illumination
of faith. We will seize the
opportunity to be enveloped
in light, and learn to face the
sunshine of revelation that is of
God. The shadows may still exist,
but they will remain behind us. The
traveling companion of iniquity is
despair, but it is because of the
Atonement that it will remain
out of sight, and out of
mind, where it cannot
harm us any more
at all.

By the Atonement, we are anchored thru Gospel topsoil into a reservoir of living water. Repentance is an expression of our honesty with ourselves, with our Father, with the Savior, and with the Holy Ghost.

Each day,
we make the
choice to repent
or not to repent,
with decisions that
we pray to God will
be illuminated by our
testimony of the power
of the Atonement, that
intuitively will draw us
closer to godlike traits
that cause us to shrink
from sin and even to
view it as something
that is repulsive
to our spirits.

The Spirit of God expands our vision to embrace the doctrine of Atonement that relates to time as well as to eternity. Subsequently, if we refuse to seize upon our opportunity to repent, we become insensitive to the better angels of our nature and we lose our ability to figuratively touch and tangibly feel its influence with a spiritual sixth sense.

In between the sights and sounds, rides and attractions, and thrills and spills of our earthly theme-park experience on the carousel of life, it is the Atonement that teaches us to use spiritual hygiene practices to remove the grit and grime that always threaten to foul our inner workings. These are the carnival barkers and flim-flam artists, whose sole mission in life seems to be to slow our progress on the pathway to perfection.

The Atonement allows us to overcome our selfishness, and our indefensible desire to be shown Mercy without Justice, which is nothing more than a doctrine of the Devil.

The Savior is our Advocate with the Father, and is the Bread of Life, the Foundation of faith beneath our existence, and the Cornerstone of our belief. He is the Deliverer of the everlasting covenant, and in His Atonement, He is the Author of our salvation.

If we
wish to have
the faith to be
saved by the power
of the Atonement of
Christ, we must keep our
eyes fixed on the prize, as
we reach out beyond our
comfort zones to snatch
the golden ring that
hangs beside the
carousel of
life.

The
Atonement
helps us catalyze
our feeling, capture
our emotion, contour
our attitude, crystallize
thought, congeal passion,
compartmentalize action
and convey sentiment,
that lead to spiritual
revitalization.

The only payment required for the gift of salvation is the heart and a willing mind. The Atonement means that sin is the only thing that we must give up, to inherit eternal life.

If we ignore the Atonement, we cannot ever hope to superficially whitewash our sins to cover them up, no matter how hard we try.

The Atonement has purpose and meaning only for those who are willing to sacrifice their broken heart and contrite spirit to the Savior of the world.

In
lieu
of the
Sacrament,
and if we do
not repent, the
Holy Spirit, which
has the capacity to
burn as a fire, must
be quenched, as the
Atonement fades in
its power to save
us from our
sins.

At times,
the power of
the Atonement
needs to be felt
through suffering.
As Paul wrote: "For
unto you it is given
in behalf of Christ,
not only to believe
on him, but also
to suffer for
his sake."

The invitation to forgive and to be forgiven is juxtaposed against the sense of despair, despondency, misery, and desperation that often is a part of our mortal schooling. The Savior's Atonement is a beacon of hope in a confusing world where opposition is everywhere.

Lucifer fell from heaven with a deafening thud. We feel its after-shock even today, as our knees shake under the weight of sin. It is only in the Atonement that we can find the strength to stand tall and not topple over.

The Spirit extends to us the promise of a wonderful opportunity to enjoy the bliss of His abode in heaven. Because of the Atonement, we will relish the warm embrace of Heavenly Father, His Son Jesus Christ, and the Holy Ghost.

The virtues of conformity to the requirements of the Atonement are a well-trained mind, a body to match, a love of achievement, and focused faith. Without these, life can be nothing more than smoke and mirrors, and we grow old before our time.

There is no revelation where there is no student, and if we do not ask the right questions that relate to the Atonement of Jesus Christ, we will be at odds with our faith. We will be doomed to receive the wrong answers. Sadly, rational minds will never be able to bridge the gap that must exist between the profane character of the worldly-wise and the divine nature.

Blessed
are they who,
when they face
temptation, have
the faith to turn to
the right. It is by the
Holy Ghost that they
will be shown how to
negotiate their way
past the doctrinal
detours and the
telestial traffic
that block the
path to the
Atonement
of Christ.

Faith is impotent when it does not lead us to grasp the Savior's Atonement, and to make the connection between it and the divine design that exists for each one of us.

Repentance can catalyze our relationship with God when it unshackles us from the icy grip of our captivity to Satan. All is because of the Atonement of Christ.

Some may ask: "What do I want out of life?" but those who have faith in the Atonement of Jesus Christ ask: "What would my Savior have me do?"

When
we stand
before God
on the Day of
Judgment, we can
be uncompromised by
corruption. Repentance
is one of those things in
life that seems almost too
good to be true, but what
does make it believable
is our abiding faith in
the miracle of the
Atonement.

The
Atonement
grounds us to a
practical belief, even
as its elements commit
us to an upward thrust.
The Spirit confirms that
we are known to God
and to the angels in
heaven who, even
now, are quietly
taking note of
everything we
think and
say and
do.

The Atonement of Christ is as a dowry from Deity that is designed to foster our faith in the financial stability of His treasury, and facilitate unwavering fidelity to Him who serves as Chief Financial Officer of Heaven.

Knowledge that has been acquired through the exercise of faith is a mortar that joins together the building blocks of testimony and conversion. It can bind us to the Atonement of Christ.

The Devil urges us to follow his detours from the strait and narrow path, that will lead us through telestial traffic, conceptual cul-de-sacs, religious roundabout, and doctrinal dead ends, from which escape is possible only through the Atonement of Christ.

Christ's Atonement nurtures our relationship with God and the Spirit, freeing us to become the fashioners of our fortunes, even as we learn to rely upon resources that are greater than ourselves.

The Atonement is a catalyst that propels us upward toward the discovery of personal levels of our experience with the Savior. Doctrine can only be tested if we nurture a companionship with the Spirit. When we fall under its spell, we are at-one with the Savior of the world.

Baptism
can catalyze
our relationship
with God when it
shatters the icy grip
of our captivity to
Satan; and all is
because of the
Atonement
of Christ.

Whenever we are spiritually neglectful, drastic action is required. The plastic surgery of the Atonement is indicated if we want to experience a reversal of our fortunes and if we hope to restore the likeness and image of our Father to countenances that have been blemished by unresolved sin.

Without our
resolute repentance
that is founded upon a
correct understanding of
the Atonement, we cannot
reasonably expect to inherit
the glory of celestial realms;
especially if we have aforetime
been agreeable to abide by only
telestial or terrestrial principles
that put fewer demands upon
our discipleship.

If we
do not beg for
our own forgiveness,
and if we do not forgive
those who have purportedly
trespassed against us, we will
find that we are trapped in the
spiritual vacuum of sin-bound
souls. We will be gasping for
air while only inches away
from the rescue of the
Atonement of Jesus
Christ.

The Atonement encourages us to constantly strive to do more, to be better, to seek understanding, and to become empowered by wisdom. We emulate the Olympic motto: "Citius, Altius, Fortius," that is to say, "Faster, Higher, Stronger."

The beauty of repentance, that is made possible by the Atonement of Jesus Christ, is that it is a primer on midwifery, with the Savior our labor coach, as we begin the arduous birthing process of our reunion with God that He characterizes as being born again.

Because of the Atonement, as we complete the process of repentance, we experience feelings of harmony and the stirrings of serenity, in ways that have been delightfully designed by our Father in Heaven to give us pause and touch our heart strings.

Silently,
the Atonement
teaches powerful
doctrine. It gives us
the means to suppress the
natural inclinations of the
telestial world that surround
us, continually encroaching
upon our spiritual stability,
and threatening to erode
our testimony of Gospel
principles that relate
to forgiveness.

We are on the
path that leads to
celestial glory if we
accept inspired direction
with dedicated purpose. Our
discipleship is actively linked
to faithful consistency in our
reliance upon the Atonement.
These will bless us with the
revelatory guidance we
need to find our way
back to our home
in heaven.

As we pass
thru the portal
of baptism, our lives
open up in an expansion
of eternal opportunities as we
obtain the remission of our sins
through the Atonement of Christ,
gain membership in the Church,
and are personally sanctified
as we receive the gift of the
Holy Ghost. We have the
Spirit of God to be
with us.

Powerful
forces constantly
refine us by pushing
and pulling at us within
the crucible of experience.
During the process, we can't
eliminate the consequences of
actions that are less than perfect.
For that to happen, our Heavenly
Father has provided us with the
Atonement of Christ; He Who
was the Lamb slain from
before the foundation
of the world.

Weakness can seed the atmosphere of our inspiration, to moisten and nurture our tender testimonies as well as to germinate our budding desire to repent of our wicked ways by taking full advantage of the Atonement of Christ.

The
Atonement
is the initiator
of a constructive
process that has been
designed to build us up,
even if it has to first tear
us down. It is involved with
recovery, to be sure. But
its primary focus is
on discovery.

The
power of
the Atonement
is nurtured within
the rich culture medium
of faith, validated by baptism
in a metaphysical reunion with
God. It is witnessed in the fiery
cauldron of the Spirit, and we
follow its glowing path in
the hope that we will be
ransomed from
our sins.

Perfect repentance, that is witnessed by the Spirit of Justification, is based on the Atonement, and compels us to consider the possibility that, by the grace of God, we might one day actually be holy and without spot, as is our Lord and Savior.

If
we try
to shirk the
demands that the
Spirit places upon us,
we risk being swallowed
up by a leviathan no less
real than that experienced
by Jonah. We can then only
expect to be spit out upon
the sandy white beach of
the covenants we have
aforetime made
with God.

The world seeks change by exerting external controls, and fails miserably. The Spirit influences the inner vessel, and succeeds brilliantly. He does this by recalibrating our internal compass so that we might remain oriented toward the Atonement of Christ.

In matters of faith, altitude is all about attitude. When we stay focused on The Plan, we raise our sights, so that we are always looking looking up, in the direction of our dreams.

The Atonement of the Son of God emboldens us with hope, and it blesses us with the fortitude to be able to endure. It motivates us to seek after anything that is lovely, or of good report, or praiseworthy.

Our own forgiveness can serve as a pacemaker that regulates the steady rhythm of the therapeutic pulses of the doctrinal energy that is found in the Atonement of Christ.

Even when the
raw feelings of pride
have tainted and twisted
our character, our salvation
lies in the Atonement. When
we look around us to argue
who is right, repentance
stands ready to look
up to God to ask
what is right.

No matter how ponderous the burdens are that we have created due to our inattention to our spiritual well-being, Jesus Christ, Who is the Savior of the world and is the Mediator of the Atonement, will lift us up at the last day.

Perhaps it is
only when we have
hit rock-bottom, that
we hear an awful noise
ringing in our ears, as the
whole earth groans under
the ponderous weight of
sin, in the absence of
an Atonement that
we must be ready
to accept.

Death is
our golden ticket
that reintroduces us
to the secret garden of
our primeval childhood,
and to the wonders of
eternity that lie in
wait just beyond
the Atonement
of Christ.

Our Lord Jesus Christ taught that we must be perfect, for otherwise we cannot inherit the Kingdom of God. Perhaps He meant that we must strive to be perfect in our repentance, in the same way that He was perfect in His Atonement.

The Atonement of Jesus Christ will bless us to enjoy a sense of permanency and strength, while the baubles of Babylon are nothing more than a bribery and a cheap trick. They are the opposites of the Savior's promise to the faithful of the incorruptible riches of eternity.

The
Gospel
sets us free to
be creative, and
sets us creative to
become more free, by
unleashing the doctrine
of the Atonement and
releasing it so it
can work its
magic.

The
Atonement
asks us to ignore
our natural instincts,
and to put our trust in
the Savior of the world,
who will lead us to the
highlands of the
morning.

A wonderful benefit of the Atonement is that we will receive the strength to endure the suffering that is part of life, but that is not of our own doing.

About The Author

Phil Hudson and his wife Jan have 7 children and over 25 grandchildren. They enjoy spending time with their family at their cabin nestled in the Selkirk Mountains, on the shore of Priest Lake, the crown jewel of North Idaho. Phil had a successful dental practice in Spokane, Washington for 43 years, before retiring in 2015. He has an eclectic mix of hobbies, and enjoys the out of doors. He always finds time, however, to record his thoughts on his laptop, and understands Isaac Asimov's response when he was asked: If you knew that you had only 10 minutes left to live, what would you do?" He answered: "I'd type faster."

Phil received the inspiration to write this book while he and Jan were serving as missionaries for The Church of Jesus Christ of Latter-day Saints, in the Kingdom of Tonga. While there, they celebrated their 50th wedding anniversary.

It is our faith in the
Atonement of Jesus Christ that
compels us to trust God's divine
design, and not devilish doctrines.
The Plan invites us to believe that
our lives are "fairy tales that
are waiting to be written
by the hand of God."
(H.C. Anderson).

By The Author

Essays

    Volume One: Spray From The Ocean Of Thought
    Volume Two: Ripples On A Pond
    Volume Three: Serendipitous Meanderings
    Volume Four: Presents Of Mind
    Volume Five: Mental Floss
    Volume Six: Fitness Training For The Mind And Spirit

First Principles and Ordinances Series

    Faith - Our Hearts Are Changed
    Repentance - A Broken Heart and a Contrite Spirit
    Baptism - One Hundred And One Reasons Why We Are Baptized
    The Holy Ghost - That We Might Have His Spirit To Be With Us
    The Sacrament - This Do In Remembrance Of Me

Book of Mormon Commentary

    Volume One: Born In The Wilderness
    Volume Two: Voices From The Dust
    Volume Three: Journey To Cumorah

Doctrine & Covenants Commentary

    Volume One - Sections 1 - 34
    Volume Two - Sections 35 - 57

Minute Musings: Spontaneous Combustions of Thought

    Volume One
    Volume Two
    Volume Three

Calendars:

    In His Own Words: Discovering William Tyndale
    As I Think About The Savior
    Scriptural Symbols

Children's Books

    Muddy, Muddy
    The Thirteen Articles of Faith
    Happy Birthday

Doctrinal Themes

    The House of the Lord

A Thought For Each Day of the Year

    Faith
    Repentance
    Baptism
    The Holy Ghost
    The Sacrament
    The House of the Lord
    The Plan of Salvation
    The Atonement
    Revelation
    The Sabbath
    Life's Greatest Questions

Professional Publications

    Diode Laser Soft Tissue Surgery Volume One
    Diode Laser Soft Tissue Surgery Volume Two
    Diode Laser Soft Tissue Surgery Volume Three

These, and other titles, are available from online retailers.

In a perfect
storm of our belief,
faith, and knowledge, it
is the light of Atonement that
switches on as a bright star in the
heavens, as if it utilizes a hydrogen
fuel to power the chain reaction of
a nuclear furnace in the center
of the cosmos.

Quid magis possum dicere?

www.ingramcontent.com/pod-product-compliance
Lightning Source LLC
Chambersburg PA
CBHW082107280426
43661CB00090B/952